Noun Hounds
& Other Great Grammar Games

20 Fun and Easy Reproducible Games That Help Every Kid Grasp the Essential Rules of Grammar

By Lorraine Hopping Egan

SCHOLASTIC

PROFESSIONAL BOOKS

New York • Toronto • London • Auckland • Sydney • Mexico City • New Delhi • Hong Kong

Dedication

To Megan A., Bianca B., Jennifer C., Dominic D., Ondrena E., Tina E.,
Jessica H., David H., Corrie K., Kiaira M., Danielle O., Kevin S.,
Sarah Z.—my hardworking game testers—
and their relentless (in a nice way) leader, Mrs. Spigarelli

Cover and interior design by
Holly Grundon

Illustrations by
Dave Clegg

ISBN 0-439-05174-6

Contents

Contents

Introduction

Classroom Strategies and Suggestions for Success

Grammar is one of those Teflon subjects: It often doesn't stick no matter how many times you teach it.

The grammar games in this book can truly help. They're more than just fun and motivational. The games present grammar skills in a variety of contexts so that students can immediately apply what they are learning. They also accommodate a range of learning styles and number of players, from solitaire games to large groups. (See chart, page 8.)

Here are a few of the exciting roles that your game players will play:
- robots that follow precise imperative verbs to carry out simple tasks ("Command Performance," page 16)

- actors who act out adverbs by the way they walk ("Walk the Walk," page 39)

- playful puppeteers who use cut-out figures to demonstrate prepositions ("Where's Herman?," page 42)

- penny-wise merchants who bid for correctly punctuated sentences ("Pearls of Wisdom," page 50)

- secret-code crackers who correct capitalization to decipher the punch line to a joke ("Crack Me Up!," page 67)

- newspaper editors who clean up copy on deadline ("The Write Rules," page 62, and "The Drop Deadline Grammar Slammer Game," page 89)

Herman

Mixed Abilities and Multi-Level Play

All of the games include suggestions for simplifying or increasing the challenge of the game play or subject matter. (See "Other Ways to Play" at the end of each game.) These variations allow beginning students to succeed at and then build on skills as they play games over and over.

Many games allow beginning and advanced students to play together competitively. For example, in "Noun Hounds" (page 13), a favorite among game testers, players name nouns that begin with certain letters. Beginners can name any noun, while more advanced students can choose a category of noun, such as places. Other games provide multiple sets of game materials on different ability levels.

After each game-playing session, invite students to share their strategies for winning and offer their own rule variations.

Deciding Who Goes First

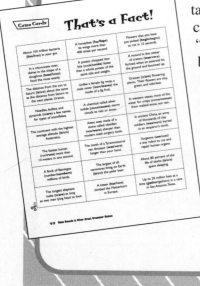

The game "Agreeable Facts" (page 19) instructs players to take turns in order of their birthdays—first to last in the calendar year. For other games, a simple variation of "Noun Hounds" provides a way to decide who goes first based on skill rather than luck. Moving clockwise around the circle of players (or back and forth between two players), students must quickly name a noun that begins with the last letter of a previously named noun. The first player is the youngest player. He or she starts with the word *noun*. A typical round would go something like this: *noun, name, elephant, tree, easel, light,* and so on. The first player to hesitate or miss goes last. The player to his or her left goes first, with play proceeding clockwise.

Advancing Around a Game Board

Flipping a coin to advance can be awkward for young children. Instead, have the person on the player's left hide the coin (or other small object) in either hand behind his or her back, and then hold out both fists. The player whose turn it is picks a fist. If the fist does not contain the coin, the player moves one space; if it does contain the coin, the player moves two spaces.

Storing Games for Future Use

Once you have assembled a game, you can easily store it in a large envelope or a file folder. Here's a tip: Glue laminated game boards (or enlargements of the game boards) to the inside of a file folder. Make sure the folder lays reasonably flat on a desk or table. Glue the game rules on the other side of the folder. Place game pieces or cards in a small envelope and store the envelope inside the modified folder. When you're ready to play, simply pull out the folder, open it, and begin!

Applying the Games to Your Learners

Grammar Game	Number of Players				Learning Style						
	1 Player	2 to 4 Players	Small Group	Large Group	Verbal	Logical	Visual/Spatial	Kinesthetic (bodily)	Rhythmic	Interpersonal (team)	Intrapersonal (alone)
1. The Nouns We Found*	●	●	●	●	●	●				●	●
2. Noun Hounds		●			●						●
3. Command Performance*			●	●	●	●		●		●	
4. Agreeable Facts			●		●	●		●			●
5. Time Travel	●	●			●						●
6. Black Hole Pronouns		●			●						●
7. Hinky Pinky Adjectives			●	●	●					●	●
8. Walk the Walk*			●	●	●		●	●	●	●	
9. Where's Herman?		●	●		●			●		●	
10. Word Buzz	●	●	●	●	●				●	●	●
11. Pearls of Wisdom		●	●	●	●	●				●	
12. Compound Your Luck*		●	●	●	●			●			●
13. Run-On Riddle Relay			●	●	●	●		●		●	
14. The Write Rules*	●	●	●	●	●						●
15. Crack Me Up!	●	●	●	●	●	●					●
16. Word Jam Concentration			●	●	●			●		●	●
17. Cooking Up Plurals		●			●						●
18. Sound Sisters		●			●						●
19. Seven-Up Spelling		●			●						●
20. Drop Deadline*	●	●	●	●	●					●	●

*Cooperative rules or variations

The Nouns We Found Word Challenge

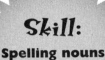

Skill:

Spelling nouns and pronouns from a set of letters

Players:

Any number of pairs or individuals

Materials:

❋ Rules of the Game (page 10)

❋ Meatball Sandwich Letter Cards (page 12)

❋ Envelope (one for each pair)

❋ Pencil

❋ Clock or timer

The Game in a Nutshell

Pairs of students have a limited amount of time to spell as many nouns as they can from the letters in the key words *meatball sandwich*.

Preparation

Divide the class into pairs. Photocopy the Rules of the Game for each pair. Choose one of the following key words according to the class's ability level (from easier to harder): *sandwich, meat sandwich,* or *meatball sandwich*. For each pair of students, photocopy the letters in your key word onto oak tag, cut them apart, and place them in an envelope. Students will rearrange these letters to form words.

Basic Grammar Skills

Ask students: What is a *noun*? *(A word that is a name, place, or thing)* How do you know when a word is a noun?

One test is to place an article, such as *the, a,* or *an,* in front of the word: *the car* works, but *the go* or *the red* doesn't. *Car* is a noun; *go* and *red* aren't. This method isn't foolproof—*the happiness* works, but it may sound awkward until you put it in a sentence: *The happiness that they felt lasted for minutes.*

Another test is to try placing a verb after the word: *The car drives* (sounds good!) versus *The red drives* (makes no sense).

A third, more sophisticated test is to replace the word with a pronoun—if you can do it, the word is a noun. For example, *happiness* can be replaced by *it,* but *drives* (a verb) cannot.

Other Ways to Play

Advanced Scoring: To encourage students to look for less obvious words, cross out all nouns that appear on more than one list. For example, if *wand* appears on two teams' lists, neither team can score points for it. Score as usual for words that appear on only one list.

Verb Version: Instead of nouns, challenge teams to list verbs in the present tense. Point out that some nouns (*will, hide, swell,* and so on) can also be verbs.

Anagrams on the Web: Students can use the following Web sites to get an instant list of *anagrams* (words that have all the letters of another word, such as *sandwich,* but in different order), and determine which ones are nouns:
www.anagramfun.com/cgi-bin/anagrams.cgi
www.wordsmith.org/anagram/index.html

Name: _____

The Nouns We Found

**Spell as many nouns as you can
from the letters in an envelope.**

How to Play:

1. Open the envelope your teacher gave you.
On the back of this page, list as many common
nouns and pronouns as you can from the letters in
the envelope. The rules:
- No plural nouns or proper nouns.
- The longer the word, the more points awarded
  (see "Scoring," below).
- Players who use every letter in the envelope
  are automatic winners.

2. When time is up, add up your score. Teams with
the highest scores or who use every letter to form
a word win.

Players:

**Any number
of pairs or
individuals**

Materials:

✳ Envelope with
letters (from
your teacher)

✳ Pencil

Scoring

0 points for words
that are not nouns, are
proper nouns, or are
plurals

1 point for each noun
with four letters or fewer

3 points for each
five-letter noun

5 points for each
six-letter noun

10 points for each
noun with seven or more
letters

The Nouns We Found

Here are some of the nouns and pronouns found in *meatball sandwich*.

Add your students' original nouns to this master list.

One letter:
I

Two letters:
ad, he, it, me, we

Three letters:
aim, ale, ant, ash, awe, bat, bet, dab, dam, end, hat, hem, lab, law, saw, sea, she, tab, tic, tie

Four letters:
ache, ante, bail, bait, bale, ball, band, bane, beam, beat, bell, bile, bill, bite, call, cast, chat, chin, chit, clam, dash, date, dell, dial, dime, dish, hail, hall, hand, hide, hill, inch, item, lamb, lane, lash, lawn, line, mail, male, mall, mane, mate, math, mean, meat, mile, mill, mist, mite, nail, name, sail, sand, seam, seat, side, sill, slab, stem, swim, team, tide, tile, time, wall, wand, wash, well, whim, will, wind, wish

Five letters:
antic, batch, beast, blame, cable, claim, chain, chase, cheat, chill, chime, clash, climb, clime, dance, ditch, label, lance, latch, lathe, match, media, sable, scale, shale, shame, slime, stain, stall, stand, steam, still, swain, sweat, swell, swill, swine, table, twill, whale, wheat, winch, witch

Six letters:
ballet, candle, castle, denial, handle, mallet, mantle, median, stable, wallet

Seven letters:
ballast, climate, machine, swindle, thimble, whistle

Eight letters:
claimant, laminate, mandible

Nine letters:
malachite

Students' original words:

_____

_____

_____

_____

_____

_____

_____

_____

The Nouns We Found

M	E	A	T	B	A	L	L
S	A	N	D	W	I	C	H
M	E	A	T	B	A	L	L
S	A	N	D	W	I	C	H
M	E	A	T	B	A	L	L
S	A	N	D	W	I	C	H
M	E	A	T	B	A	L	L
S	A	N	D	W	I	C	H

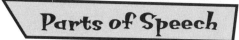

Noun Hounds Board Game

Skill:

Identifying nouns

Players:

2 to 4

Materials:

✳ Rules of the Game (page 14)

✳ Noun Hounds game board and playing pieces (page 15)

✳ Pencil

The Game in a Nutshell

Players race from *A* to *Z*, naming nouns that begin with certain letters.

Preparation

Photocopy and enlarge the game board. Cut out the playing pieces along the dotted lines, then fold along the solid lines so pieces can stand on their own. Distribute one playing piece to each player. Photocopy the Rules of the Game for each player.

For more than two players, students should elect a *timekeeper* (to count out three seconds on each turn) and a *recorder* (to list nouns generated during game play). A third player will count out the seconds during the timekeeper's turn.

For instructions on how to decide who goes first, see page 6.

Basic Grammar Skills

"Noun Hounds" are players who can easily sniff out a noun when they need one. Nouns are people, places, or things (including ideas, such as *happiness*). Ask students to provide examples of each type of noun.

Other Ways to Play

Noun Categories: Specify a category of nouns—person, place, or thing—for players to name.

Geography Nouns: For geography practice, players must name a proper noun that's a place (*Arizona, Boise, Canada*).

Career Nouns: A career variation challenges children to name a person that is a common noun (*artist, baseball player, car dealer*).

Science Nouns: Expand science vocabulary by having children name common or proper nouns that are plants (*apple tree, birch, cauliflower*), animals (*albatross, baboon, caribou*), or minerals (*amethyst, basalt, calcium*).

Nouns and Verbs: In five seconds, players name words that are both nouns and verbs (*act, cut, drink*).

Name: _____

Noun Hounds

As you race from A to Z, name nouns that begin with the letter you land on.

How to Play:

1. Place the Noun Hounds game pieces on START.

2. To start your turn, move your piece forward to the next empty (or unoccupied) space.

3. When you land on a letter, you have three seconds to name a noun that begins with that letter. The time-keeper quietly counts, "One noun hound, two noun hound, three noun hound," and then says, "Time!"

4. If you correctly name a noun in time, stay in place. The recorder writes down the noun on the back of this page, and your turn ends. If you can't name a noun, or if you say a non-noun or a noun that has already been mentioned, go back to the nearest empty space and wait for your next turn. (Ignore any instructions or letters on the space.)

5. The first player to reach Z and name a noun that starts with Z in three seconds wins.

Players:
2 to 4

Materials:

✳ Noun Hounds game board and playing pieces

✳ Pencil

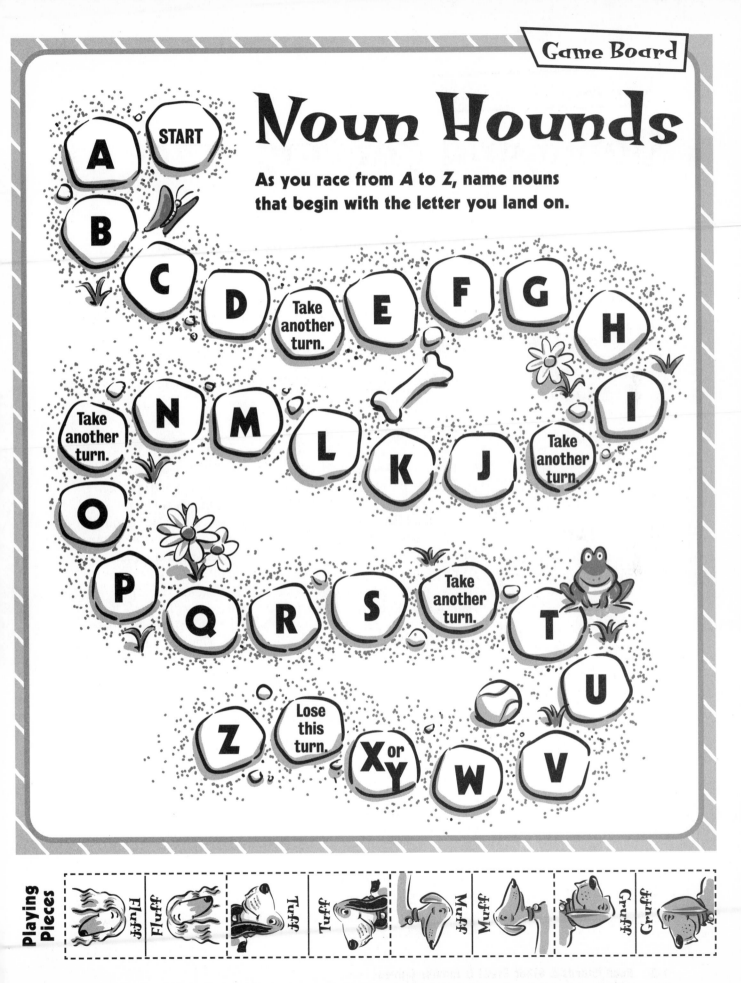

Noun Hounds

As you race from *A* to *Z*, name nouns that begin with the letter you land on.

START

A
B
C
D

Take another turn.

E
F
G
H
I

Take another turn.

N
M
L
K
J

Take another turn.

O
P
Q
R
S

Take another turn.

T
U

Z

Lose this turn.

X or Y
W
V

Playing Pieces

Fluff   Fluff   Tuff   Tuff   Muff   Muff   Gruff   Gruff

Command Performance

Players:

Any number of teams of 2 to 6 students

Materials:

* Rules of the Game (page 17)

* Robot Task Cards (page 18)

* Paper and pencils

* Props (optional)

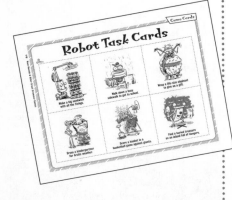

The Game in a Nutshell

Each team uses precise imperative verbs to write a *program*—step-by-step instructions—for "robots" to carry out.

Preparation

Divide the class into teams of 2 to 6 students. Encourage students to give their teams robotic names, such as The Chipsters, Dream Machines, or Robot Rooters. Provide each team with a copy of the Rules of the Game, scrap paper, and pencils.

Photocopy the Robot Task Cards and cut them apart. Give each team a Task Card and simple props.

Basic Grammar Skills

Verbs are action words that give nouns something to do. Plain verbs, such as *has, is, go,* and *do,* are ordinary and somewhat vague. Verbs such as *jump, slurp,* and *finish* are more interesting and specific.

To help students generate precise verbs, play a warm-up round of "Command Performance" in which the class writes a program for a robot to make a banana milkshake. Omit certain steps to encourage students to think through the process logically and completely.

Write the ordinary verb *make* on the board. Ask: What more precise verbs describe making a shake? Brainstorm a list: *peel, chop, smash, blend, churn, mix, open, drop, shake, pour, flip,* etc. Organize the words into a program using verbs in the *imperative* (command) mood and add an object noun after the verb. Here's a sample program:

1 Lift lid (of blender)
2 Peel banana
3 Cut banana
4 Drop banana (in blender)
5 Open milk carton
6 Lift milk carton
7 Pour milk (in blender)
8 Flip switch

Have volunteer "robots" check how well the program has been written by acting out the steps. Emphasize that robots can't change their programs; they can only do exactly what their program tells them to do.

Discuss the results: Did anything go wrong? Are steps missing or unclear? For example, the program didn't say to replace the lid on the blender before flipping on the switch. How could students improve this program?

Other Way to Play

Adverb Extension: Encourage advanced players to add an adverb to each step of the command. For example, *chop banana finely* or *replace lid tightly.*

Team: _____

Command Performance

Use precise verbs to write a *program* (step-by-step instructions) for "robots" to carry out.

How to Play:

1. There are no winners or losers in "Command Performance." The goal is to come up with a list of *imperative* (command) verbs in logical order so that others can follow your program.

2. Read the Robot Task your teacher gave you. You and your team have a limited time* to write a robot program to carry out the task. Begin by brainstorming a list of precise imperative verbs. Then, organize your verbs into a step-by-step program and write it on the back of this page. TIP: Rehearse your program to iron out any bugs.

3. Exchange programs with another team. Take turns acting out the other team's program silently with or without props. Team members should alternate steps so that everyone gets a chance to follow a command. Remember: Robots can't add to or change their programs to correct errors or omissions.

4. After each performance, discuss the results. How could you improve the other team's program? What other verbs would you use to describe actions?

*Teacher: Set your own time limit, from 5 to 10 minutes.

Players:
Any number of teams of 2 to 6 students

Materials:
* Robot Task Card (from your teacher)
* Paper and pencil
* Props (optional)
* Watch or timer

Robot Task Cards

Wrap a life-size elephant
to give as a gift.

Find a buried treasure
on an island full of dangers.

Walk down a busy
sidewalk to get to school.

Score a basket in a
basketball game against giants.

Make a big sandwich
with all the fixings.

Dress a kindergartner
for Arctic weather.

Agreeable Facts Relay Race

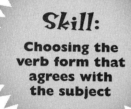

Skill:
Choosing the verb form that agrees with the subject

Players:
4 to 6

Materials:
* Rules of the Game (page 20)
* That's a Fact! Cards (pages 21–23)

The Game in a Nutshell
Each player reads a science fact with two verb forms. Other players must choose the verb that agrees with the subject to earn points.

Preparation
Photocopy the Fact Cards onto oak tag and cut them apart. Laminate the cards for longer use. Photocopy the Rules of the Game for players.

Basic Grammar Skills
The science facts listed on the cards are true, but only one of the two verb forms—the one in boldface—agrees with the subject. Have students practice classifying the subject nouns on several of the cards as either singular or plural.

When nouns of quantity (*nine Martians*), distance (*three miles*), time (*two years*), and amount (*a million dollars*) count as a unit, they are singular. For example: *Twenty years is the average life span of a lion.*

Collective nouns that name a group of people, places, or things are singular: *A class of 25 students is very likely to have two birthdays on the same day.*

Pronouns such as *either, somebody, nobody, everything,* and *anybody* are always singular. Example: *Everybody warms up a little bit during the dream stage of sleep.*

For more practice with pronouns, see "Black Hole Pronoun," page 29.

Other Ways to Play
Tough Bluff: In this strategic version, the reader chooses one verb form (either correct or incorrect) in the parentheses and reads aloud the sentence, inserting the chosen verb form. The player at the front of the line either agrees or disagrees with the choice of verb form. If the player is correct, he or she becomes the new reader.

Social Studies Twist: Add history and geography facts to the cards.

Agreeable Facts Relay Race

In sentences with facts, decide which verb agrees with the subject.

How to Play:

1. The player whose birthday falls earliest in the year is the first reader. Other players line up in front of the reader in order of their birthdays.

2. Shuffle the cards and place them facedown on a table. The reader draws the top card, taking care not to show it to the other players. The reader reads the sentence aloud twice, each time inserting a different verb form from the parentheses. (The correct verb form is in **boldface**.)

3. The first player in line guesses the correct verb form:

- If correct, the player keeps the card and becomes the new reader. The former reader goes to the end of the line.

- If the player is incorrect, he or she goes to the end of the line. The reader puts the card in a discard pile and draws a second card to read to the next player in line.

4. Play continues in this way until the game ends in one of two ways:

- One reader stumps all the other players in a row and so wins the game.

- The cards are all used up, and the winner is the player with the most cards.

5. For the next round of play, the player whose birthday falls second in the year goes first. The first reader from the first game goes last.

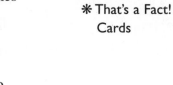

Players:
4 to 6

Materials:

❋ That's a Fact! Cards

That's a Fact!

The total height of three men (equal/**equals**) the height of one adult giraffe.

The cause of goosebumps (**is**/are) your muscles squeezing the base of your body hairs.

The hearts of Brachiosaurus dinosaurs (**were**/was) the size of pickup trucks!

Even when the outside temperature drops to 40°F, a type of lily (stay/**stays**) 85°F inside.

A spacesuit (contain/**contains**) 11 or more different layers of material.

When pockets of air (**bump**/bumps) against food in your stomach, your stomach "growls."

Cooties are a type of louse, a parasite that (live/**lives**) on humans.

A blue whale (hear/**hears**) other blue whales up to 500 miles away.

Both a rat and a beaver (**grind**/grinds) down their teeth by gnawing on things.

Everything in a landfill (**doesn't**/don't) rot.

Muscles (**create**/creates) heat by squeezing and relaxing over and over very fast, making you shiver.

Neither a rhinoceros nor a nearsighted human (see/**sees**) well far away.

The length of a blue whale (equal/**equals**) about 20 sixth graders lying head to foot in a row.

Someone (**is**/are) born in the world about three times each second on average.

Every known mountain in the solar system (**is**/are) shorter than Mount Olympus on Mars.

Somebody who exercises regularly (**is**/are) more likely to live longer.

In 1994, the planet Jupiter (**was**/were) hit by pieces of a comet.

Nothing else on Earth (stand/**stands**) higher than Mount Everest.

Nobody (live/**lives**) longer without air than without water. Humans die in minutes without oxygen.

In August 1998, the Atlantic Ocean (**was**/were) crossed by two robot airplanes without human pilots.

The taste buds of a catfish (**appear**/appears) all over its body.

Some people (**are**/is) able to roll their tongues into a "U" shape. Can you?

Everybody (**has**/have) about the same number of muscle fibers as a body builder, but the fibers of a body builder are bigger.

Both lions and house cats (**flatten**/flattens) their ears during a fight to protect themselves.

That's a Fact!

About 100 trillion bacteria (**live**/lives) in your gut.	A honeybee (flap/**flaps**) its wings more than 400 times per second.	Flowers that you have just picked (**begin**/begins) to rot in 15 seconds.
In a microwave oven, dishes in the shape of a doughnut (**heat**/heats) food the most evenly.	A potato chopped into bits (cook/**cooks**) faster than a whole potato of the same size and weight.	A mound in the center of craters (**was**/were) formed when an asteroid hit the ground and bounced up.
The distance from the sun to Saturn (**is**/are) about the same as the distance from Saturn to the next planet, Uranus.	Unlike a female fig wasp, a male never (leave/**leaves**) the inside of a fig fruit.	Grasses (is/**are**) flowering plants. Their flowers are tiny, green, and odorless.
Needles, bullets, and pyramids (is/**are**) a few names for types of snowflakes.	A chemical called silver iodide (cause/**causes**) storm clouds to rain or snow.	In western states, most of the water for crops (come/**comes**) from melted snow, not rain.
The continent with the highest average altitude (**is**/are) Antarctica.	Aztec axes made of a stone called obsidian (was/**were**) sharper than modern steel surgery tools.	In ancient China, an army of thousands of clay soldiers (**was**/were) buried in an emperor's tomb.
The fastest human (run/**runs**) more than 10 meters in one second.	The tooth of a Tyrannosaurus rex dinosaur (**was**/were) longer than your hand.	Surgeons (**use**/uses) a tiny robot to cut and repair human organs.
A flock of flamingos (number/**numbers**) millions of birds.	The largest of all carnivores living on Earth (**is**/are) the polar bear.	About 80 percent of the life of sloths (**is**/are) spent sleeping.
The longest elephant tusks (is/**are**) as long as two men lying head to foot.	A kitten (**has**/have) climbed the Matterhorn in Europe.	Up to 20 million bats at a time (**gather**/gathers) in a cave in San Antonio, Texas.

That's a Fact!

A falcon (spot/**spots**) a grasshopper from a height of six stories.	Everybody (depend/**depends**) on oxygen to survive.	Air (consist/**consists**) mostly of a gas called nitrogen, not oxygen.
At top speed, a human being (run/**runs**) a 100-meter race in about 10 seconds.	The teeth of a scared monkey (**chatter**/chatters).	About 95 percent of a head of lettuce (**is**/are) water.
A few of us (was/**were**) born with dimples, or small dents, on our face.	Unlike a butterfly, a moth (hear/**hears**) sound.	The teeth of a rodent never (**stop**/stops) growing.
Weather kites (**fly**/flies) as high as a jet.	Snakes (**taste**/tastes) the air with their long, forked tongues.	Either the wing or the foot of a fly (taste/**tastes**) foods with special sensors.
Unlike crawling lizards, alligators (**lift**/lifts) their bellies off the ground when they run.	The American alligator (**is**/are) no longer on the endangered-species list.	Cockroaches eat the glue binding in books if better food (**is**/are) not available.
Deep-ocean water (**is**/are) colder than 32°F (0°C), the freezing point of pure water.	Hurricane winds travel faster than cars on a highway, but the hurricane itself (move/**moves**) at about the speed of a bicycle.	Shooting stars (is/**are**) bits of comet dust burning up in Earth's atmosphere.
Falcons can spot a pigeon that (**is**/are) five miles away.	Like Saturn, the planets Jupiter, Uranus, and Neptune (has/**have**) rings above their equators.	Mercury, the closest planet to the sun, (travel/**travels**) faster than all the other planets.
The wing span of wandering albatrosses (equal/**equals**) two sixth graders lying head to foot.	A top pole vaulter (vault/**vaults**) over crossbars that are almost two stories high.	The most popular dog breed in the United States (**is**/are) the Labrador retriever.

Time Travel Word Maze

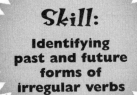

Skill:
Identifying past and future forms of irregular verbs

Players:
1 to 2

Materials:

❋ Rules of the Game (page 25)

❋ Time Travel game board (page 27)

❋ Answer Key (page 26)

❋ Dry-erase marker or grease pencil

❋ Cloth or tissue for erasing

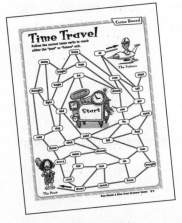

The Game in a Nutshell
Players follow either past-tense or future-tense verbs through a time machine maze to arrive at either the "past" or "future" exit.

Preparation
Make one copy of the Time Travel maze and the Rules of the Game. If possible, laminate the game board. Provide each player with a different colored dry-erase marker or grease pencil.

Basic Grammar Skills
Verbs describe actions (*walk*) or states of being (*is*). The *tense* of the verb tells when the action or state of being happened: past, present, or future.

Changing regular verbs from the present tense to the past is simple—just add *-d* or *-ed* to the verb. For example, *bake* becomes *baked* and *walk* becomes *walked*. To change present-tense verbs to the future tense, insert *will* or *shall* in front of the verb: *will bake* or *will walk*.

In the "Time Travel" game, *irregular verbs*—verbs that form their past tense in ways other than adding *-d* or *-ed*—rule the day. The game is self-checking—wrong paths end in dead ends, or pass through too many or too few words. See the Answer Key.

Other Way to Play
Time Travel Sequels: Use an enlarged copy of the Time Travel maze template (page 28) to make additional game boards. You can replace the verbs in the original game with new irregular verbs in the same tense. Another option is to replace the future-tense verbs with past participles (*begun, blown, drawn*) and rename "The Future" exit "The Past Participle."

Time Travel

**Follow the correct tense verbs to reach
either the "past" or "future" exit in a maze.**

How to Play:

1. **One person**: Choose either the past or future tense. Start at the Time Machine in the center of the maze, and draw lines to connect words that match your chosen tense. A correct path will pass through exactly 14 words and end at the matching exit, either "The Past" or "The Future." The goal is to get through the maze without making a mistake. TIP: If you choose future tense, add the word *will* before the verb to see if it sounds right.

2. **Two players**: One player chooses "past," and the other chooses "future." Players start at the Time Machine. Take turns drawing lines to the next word that matches your chosen verb tense.

3. You can challenge your opponent's move. If the other player's move is incorrect, he or she must erase the link and lose the next turn. If the challenged move is correct, you lose your next turn.

4. The first player to reach the correct exit after both players have taken an equal number of turns wins. In a perfect game (no mistakes), players will tie after 14 moves apiece.

Players:
1 or 2

Materials:
* Time Travel game board
* Dry-erase marker or grease pencil (a different color for each player)
* Cloth or tissue for erasing

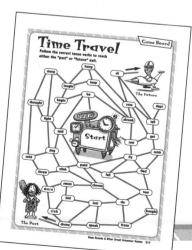

Time Travel Word List

The correct path to the Future or Past exits will pass through the boldfaced words in the matching columns below.

Future (will _____)	Simple Past	Past Participle (have or has _____)
be	was	been
begin	began	begun
fight	fought	fought
sing	sang	sung
stink	stank	stunk
choose	chose	chosen
do	did	done
tear	tore	torn
fall	fell	fallen
fly	flew	flown
catch	caught	caught
get	got	gotten
tell	told	told
sit	sat	sat
see	**saw**	seen
shrink	**shrank**	shrunk
rise	**rose**	risen
hang	**hung**	hung
teach	**taught**	taught
sting	**stung**	stung
think	**thought**	thought
sell	**sold**	sold
throw	**threw**	thrown
wear	**wore**	worn
swim	**swam**	swum
hide	**hid**	hidden
lose	**lost**	lost
drive	**drove**	driven
leap	leaped, leapt	leaped, leapt
sleep	slept	slept
lay	laid	laid
pay	paid	paid
buy	bought	bought
sink	sank	sunk
freeze	froze	frozen
speak	spoke	spoken

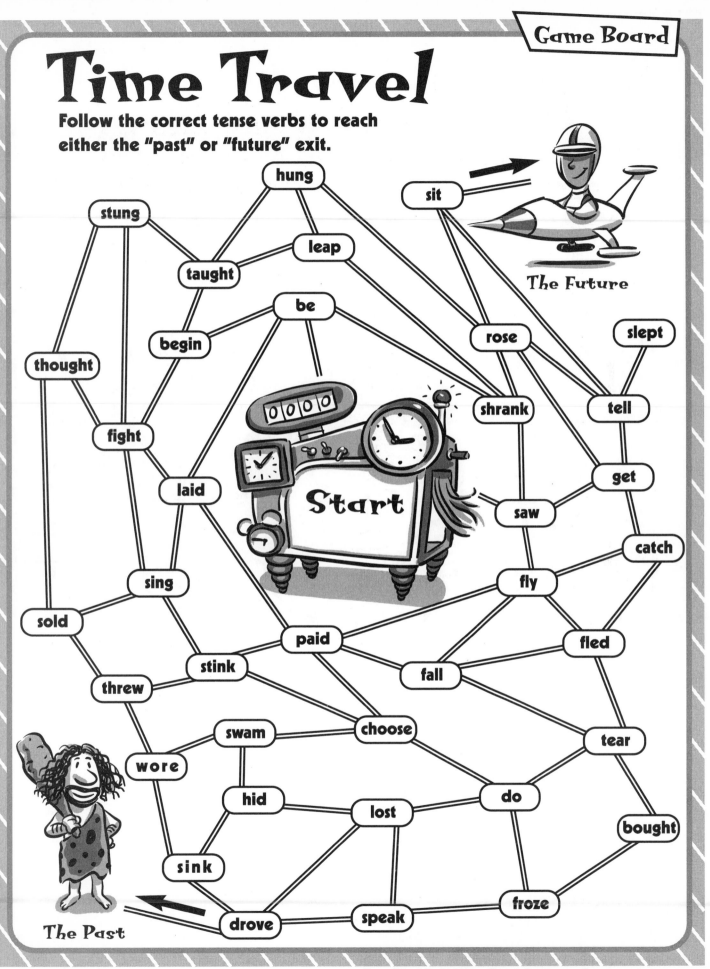

Time Travel

Follow the correct tense verbs to reach either the "past" or "future" exit.

The Future

The Past

Time Travel

Follow the correct tense verbs to reach the matching exit.

Black Hole Pronoun Game

Players:

2 to 3

Materials:

* Rules of the Game (page 30)
* Black Hole Pronoun game board (page 33)
* Black Hole poem (page 32)
* Coin or other small object
* Pencil and pen

The Game in a Nutshell

Players zoom to the center of a black hole by replacing nouns in a poem with pronouns; they zoom back out of the hole by replacing pronouns with nouns.

Preparation

Photocopy the Rules of the Game, the game board, and the poem. Cut out the playing pieces along the dotted lines, then fold along the solid lines so pieces can stand on their own. Enlarge the game board on the photocopier. Provide the playing group with a coin or other small object, and a pencil with eraser, and a pen.

If you have access to a chalkboard or dry-erase board, copy the poem onto the board, writing boldfaced words in a contrasting color. Have players erase nouns and pronouns and write in new ones in a third color of marker or chalk.

For instructions on how to decide who goes first, see page 6.

Basic Grammar Skills

Pronouns are words that can take the place of nouns. In this game the pronouns are all personal—*he, she, it, we, they*. Have students practice replacing the nouns with pronouns in the following tongue twisters:

> How much **wood** would **a woodchuck** chuck if **a woodchuck** could chuck **wood**?
> How much **of it** would **it** chuck if **it** could chuck **it**?

> **Sally and Shelly** collect **seashells** by **the seashore**.
> **They** collect **them** by **it**.

Grammar Tips

Be careful where Jerry says, "Mary and Jerry can make the reader merry." Since Jerry is speaking, replace *Mary and Jerry* with *We*.

You (players) are both *readers* and *Earthlings*. These nouns refer to the pronoun *you*.

Other Ways to Play

Simpler Version: Students can play the game going only one way—from the spaceship into the black hole. They replace nouns with pronouns until the winner reaches the center of the black hole.

Advanced Pronouns: Replace both the pronouns and nouns on the game board with more advanced pronouns such as *myself, yourself, himself, herself, itself, mine, yours, hers,* and *theirs.*

Black Hole Pronoun

**Zoom to a black hole by replacing nouns
in a poem with pronouns, and zoom back out
by replacing pronouns with nouns.**

How to Play:

1. Place the playing pieces on START. To determine how
many spaces you will move, the person on your left hides
a coin in either hand. Guess which hand holds the coin:
- If you guess correctly, move two spaces forward.
- If you guess incorrectly, move one space.
- If you land on a space already occupied by another
player, move forward to the next empty space.

2. When you land on a pronoun (on the white half of the
rocket), decide which noun in the poem it can replace.
Use the pencil to cross out the noun and write the pronoun directly above it. NOTE: Some pronouns can
replace more than one noun; the choice is up to you.
After you replace a noun and read the revised line of the
poem aloud, your turn ends.

3. If you can't find a noun to replace in the poem, go
back to the nearest empty space and wait for your next
turn. If the nearest empty space says, "Go again," take
another turn.

4. When you reach the Black Hole, stop even if you have
an extra move. Replace any boldfaced noun left in the
poem with a pronoun. If you make a mistake, you lose
your next turn. If no more nouns remain in the poem,
wait on the Black Hole for your next turn.

5. On the return trip, replace a pronoun in the poem with
the noun you land on (on the gray half of the rocket).
Use a pen to cross out the pronoun and write in the
noun. The first player to reach END wins. An exact
move is not needed.

Players:
2 or 3

Materials:

* Black Hole
  Pronouns
  game board and
  playing pieces
* Black Hole
  poem
* Coin or other
  small object
* Pencil and pen

Black Hole Pronoun

**Some nouns can be replaced by more than one pronoun
and vice versa. Here is one possible poem that doesn't rhyme—
or even make much sense. Challenge the group to rewrite it!**

....

Mary *(She/The alien girl)* **had a little lamb chop** *(it/planet)***.**

The meat *(it/rock)* **was Mary's** *(her/the alien girl's)* **own.**

Jerry *(He/The alien boy)* **ate two big pieces** *(them/the comets)*

And so did Jerry's nieces *(they/the aliens)***.**

Jerry *(He/The alien boy)* **asked more guests** *(them/the Martians)* **to dinner.**

Mary *(She/The alien girl)* **gave them a key** *(it/a rock)***.**

Jerry *(He/The alien boy)* **said, "Mary and Jerry** *(We/The Martians)*

Can make the reader *(you/the Earthling)* **merry."**

Do readers *(you/the Earthlings)* **agree with Jerry** *(him/the alien boy)***?**

Is life *(it/space)* **about everyone** *(it/the planet)* **sharing?**

Black Hole Poem

Replace the nouns with pronouns from the game board. Then, replace the pronouns with new nouns.

Mary had **a little lamb chop**.

The meat was **Mary's** own.

Jerry ate **two big pieces**

And so did **Jerry's nieces**.

Jerry asked **more guests** to dinner.

Mary gave them **a key**.

Jerry said, **"Mary and Jerry**

Can make **the reader** merry."

Do **readers** agree with **Jerry**?

Is **life** about **everyone** sharing?

Black Hole Pronoun

Use the pronoun you land on to replace a noun in the poem.
On the return trip, replace a pronoun with the noun you land on.

START / END

he / alien boy

she / alien girl

you / Earthling

we / aliens

planet / it

he / alien boy

GO AGAIN. GO AGAIN.

LOSE A TURN. GO AGAIN.

space / it

LOSE A TURN. GO AGAIN.

them / Martians

Black Hole
Stop!
Replace
any noun.

Earthling / you

alien's / her

she / alien girl

he / alien boy

GO AGAIN. GO AGAIN.

them / Martians

they / comets

him / alien boy

it / rock

Playing Pieces

Playing Pieces

Hinky Pinky Adjectives

Players:

Any number of teams with 2 or 3 students per team

Materials:

✳ Rules of the Game (page 35)

✳ Noun List 1 or 2 (pages 37–38)

✳ Pencil

✳ Rhyming dictionary (optional)

✳ Clock or timer

✳ Answer Key (page 36)

The Game in a Nutshell

Given a list of nouns (*cake*), teams vie to come up with rhyming adjectives (*fake cake*).

Preparation

Divide the class into groups of 2 or 3 students. Invite each team to choose a two-word name that rhymes, such as Dream Team or Super Grouper. Choose the Noun List that matches your students' level, and make one copy per team. Provide each group with a copy of the Rules of the Game, a pencil, and a rhyming dictionary (optional). Keep a copy of the Answer Key in front of you during the game.

Basic Grammar Skills

Adjectives are words that describe another word, usually a noun. Write the word *pie* on the board and ask students to write down answers the following questions:

- What color is it?
- How big is it?
- What shape is it?
- How does it smell?
- How many are there?
- How else can you describe it?

Compare students' answers. How many different adjectives answer each question? Have students use their adjectives in sentences: *The three juicy pies smelled lemony and tasted tangy.*

Have students count the syllables in their adjectives. A one-syllable adjective paired with a one-syllable rhyming noun form a "hink pink." Ask students: What hink pinks can you make for the word *pie* or *pies*? (*Dry pie, high pie, sly pie*)

Two-syllable adjective-noun pairs are "hinky pinkies." Start with the noun *lion* and brainstorm rhyming adjectives, such as *lyin' lion, cryin' lion,* and *sighin' lion.*

Other Ways to Play

Easier Edition: Instead of rhyming words, ask students to generate adjectives that begin with the same letter as each noun (*wily waiter* or *jolly jockey*)—a technique called *alliteration.*

Hinkety Pinkety: Hinkety pinketies have three syllables, such as *hard-to-reach garden peach* and *feverish licorice.* Students can also create hink pinketies (*blue saddle shoe*), hinky pinketies (*silly hillbilly*), and hinkety pinkies (*arthritic critic*).

Hinky Pinky Adjectives

Come up with adjectives that rhyme with a list of nouns.

How to Play:

1. You have limited time* to come up with rhyming adjectives to match a list of nouns.

2. List as many rhyming adjectives as you can for each noun. If you need help finding a rhyming adjective, feel free to use the definition clues. Remember to work quietly so you don't accidentally give answers to other teams.

3. When time is up, all teams should tally their points. (See "Scoring," below.) The team with the highest score wins.

Players:

Any number of teams with 2 or 3 students per team

Materials:

* Noun List (from your teacher)
* Pencil
* Rhyming dictionary (optional)
* Clock or timer

Scoring

(for Noun List 1)

3 points for each hink pink (one-syllable adjective and noun), such as *sad lad*.

2 points for each hinky pink (two-syllable adjective, one-syllable noun), such as *five-star tar*.

0 points for non-adjective words

(for Noun List 2)

3 points for each hinky pinky (two-syllable a adjective and noun), such as *hunky monkey*.

2 points for each hink pinky (one-syllable adjective, two-syllable noun): *green machine*.

0 points for non-adjective words

* Teacher: Set your own time limit, such as 10 minutes.

Hinky Pinky Adjectives

Below are some sample answers to the noun lists.

NOUN LIST 1	NOUN LIST 2
blue shoe	broken token
fat cat	surest tourist
glad lad	sharpest harpist
far tar	paler jailor
late plate	hockey jockey
meat treat	serene machine
pink sink	pocket locket
shack pack	grayer prayer
frail snail	dumber plumber
tame flame	handy candy
long song	hairy fairy
shin skin	straighter waiter
stone bone	mental rental
green queen	higher flier
loose goose	chunky monkey

Team: _____

Hinky Pinky Noun List 1

Read the list of nouns. What adjectives rhyme with these nouns? The definition clue gives you a hint for one rhyming word, but you can write as many rhyming words as you like in the first column. The more you write, the higher your score!

Adjective	Noun	Definition Clue
blue	shoe	sad footwear
	cat	chubby pet
	lad	happy boy
	tar	very distant highway
	plate	overdue dinner
	treat	juicy steak
	sink	rosy basin
	pack	group of huts
	snail	weak slow-mover
	flame	fire under control
	song	endless tune
	skin	lower-leg flesh
	bone	rock fossil
	queen	new ruler
	goose	escaped fowl

Score: _____

Team: _____

Hinky Pinky Noun List 2

Read the list of nouns. What adjectives rhyme with these nouns? The definition clue gives you a hint for one rhyming word, but you can write as many rhyming words as you like in the first column. The more you write, the higher your score!

Adjective	Noun	Definition Clue
broken	token	machine jammer
	tourist	most confident traveler
	harpist	best string plucker
	jailer	whiter warden
	jockey	ice sports radio announcer
	machine	calm robot
	locket	small watch
	prayer	less clear request
	plumber	not-so-smart pipe fitter
	candy	nearby treat
	fairy	furry Peter Pan helper
	waiter	good-postured server
	rental	lease not written on paper
	flier	soarer closer to the top
	monkey	chubby primate

Score: _____

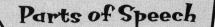

Walk the Walk Charades

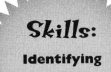
Players:

Two teams of 3 to 8 players

Materials:

✴ Rules of the Game (page 40)

✴ Walk the Walk Adverb Cards (page 41)

✴ Large envelope or paper bag

✴ Props (optional)

The Game in a Nutshell

In this variation of charades, a player walks in the style of an adverb (*secretly, gingerly, purposefully*) so that teammates can guess the adverb.

Preparation

Copy the Adverb Cards onto oak tag and cut them apart. Place the adverbs in a bag or envelope for blind drawing. Photocopy the Rules of the Game for each team.

Encourage teams to choose acting-related names, such as The Big Players, Show Stoppers, or Ham-It-Ups. Have teams choose the order in which each member will act out an adverb. You might want to provide props, such as a cane, umbrella, crown, jump rope, or cape.

Basic Grammar Skills

Just as an adjective describes a noun, an *adverb* gives more information about a verb ("adds to the verb"). As a warm-up activity, write the verb *sing* on the board. Ask students to imagine themselves singing in front of an audience and answer these questions:

- When (what time, what day) are you singing?
- For how long will you sing?
- Where are you singing?
- How fast are you singing?
- What emotions are you feeling as you sing?

List students' answers on the board and change nonadverbs into adverbs (*happy* into *happily,* for example). Invite a volunteer to choose a few adverbs from the list and demonstrate two or three different ways of singing a simple song, such as *Row, Row, Row Your Boat.*

Before playing the game, review the list of adverbs with students and discuss what each one means.

Other Ways to Play

Cooperative Play: Instead of playing in teams, draw adverbs at random and ask the whole class to act them out. Share and compare walking styles.

Multiple Verbs: Prepare a bag full of verbs: *talk, eat, dance, ride a horse, write,* and so on. Have players draw both a verb and an adverb to act out. Teammates must guess both words or their synonyms.

Walk the Walk

Guess the adverb that describes the way a teammate walks.

Players:
Two teams of 3 to 8 players

How to Play:

1. Decide in what order team members will act out the adverbs.

2. When it's your turn to act, draw an adverb from the bag. You have 60 seconds to act out the verb *walk* in the style of the adverb. As an actor, you can't speak, but you can use or pretend to use props.

3. If your teammates can guess the adverb within the time limit, your team scores two points. If they name a synonym of the adverb, your team earns one point. For example, the adverb *joyously* is synonymous with *joyfully*, *happily*, or *gladly*. If teammates fail to guess the adverb, the team gets no points for that round.

4. The other team takes a turn. Teams alternate turns until every member has had at least one chance to act. The team with the higher score wins.

Materials:

* Walk the Walk Adverb Cards (in a bag)
* Props (optional)
* Timer

Walk the Walk
Adverbs

rapidly (swiftly, fast, quickly, speedily)	**regally** (kingly, queenly, royally, nobly, majestically)
safely (carefully, cautiously)	**alertly** (watchfully, vigilantly)
secretly (slyly, covertly)	**gingerly** (lightly, quietly, gently)
casually (coolly, easily, nonchalantly, indifferently)	**painfully** (achingly, tenderly, uncomfortably)
confidently (strongly, assuredly, boldly)	**clumsily** (gawkily, awkwardly, stumblingly)
excitedly (anxiously, frantically, uncontrollably)	**competitively** (winningly, opposedly)
wondrously (in awe, admiringly)	**timidly** (scaredly, shyly, reservedly, cautiously)
joyously (joyfully, happily, gladly, gleefully, playfully)	**sadly** (sorrowfully, unhappily, gloomily, cheerlessly, dolefully)

Where's Herman? Charades

Players:

Any number of pairs, plus a game monitor

Materials:

* Rules of the Game (page 43)

* Where's Herman? Character Cards (page 45)

* Preposition Cards (page 44)

* Large envelope or paper bag

* Watch or timer

* Props

The Game in a Nutshell

One player uses stand-up figures and props to mime prepositions; the other player guesses the preposition being mimed.

Preparation

Collect a few props for players to use, such as doll furniture or toy vehicles. You can also make simple props. For example, cut a large doorway and window in a shoe box, provide rulers to use as ladders or sidewalks, gather books to serve as storied buildings or mountains, and so on.

For each pair of students, make a copy of the Rules of the Game, and two copies of the Where's Herman? Character Cards and Preposition Cards. Cut apart one set of words and place them in a bag or envelope for blind drawing. Leave the other word cards intact. Cut out the characters along the dotted lines and fold each one in half so that the pictures face out. Stand the folded figures on a table or desk with the props nearby.

Basic Grammar Skills

The *prepositions* in this game are all about location, location, location. Ask two or three student volunteers to help you demonstrate some of the words: *next to, around,* and *between.* Point out that prepositions are relative to the point of view. That is, you may be *between* two students, but the students are not *between* you; from their point of view, they are *next to* or *beside* you. In this game, Herman's point of view is the one that counts.

Allow players one or two minutes to review the word list before beginning the game. Players should pay special attention to words that are synonyms (*among* and *amid*) or similar in meaning (*in* and *inside*).

Other Ways to Play

Cooperative Version: Instead of competing against each other, pairs try to better their scores in a second round of play. After playing several rounds, challenge players to play "Where's Herman?" without the word list.

Other Prepositions: Prepositions such as *of, like, for, about, until, since, after, except,* and *during* don't indicate location. Have students use each of these words in a sentence, such as *Juan is the tallest of all the people in the class.* Then challenge students to use two prepositions in one sentence: *Except for Sheray, Juan is the tallest of all the people in the class.*

Where's Herman?

**Use character cards and props to mime prepositions,
which your partner will try to guess.**

How to Play:

1. The goal of "Where's Herman?" is to act out and guess as many prepositions as possible in two minutes. Decide who will be the first actor and who will be the first guesser. The actor takes the cut-out words and characters; the guesser uses the word list for reference. Players switch roles after one minute.

2. To start, the game monitor says, "Where's Herman?" and begins timing the action. Actors randomly draw a word card, read it silently, and place it facedown. Actors then use the character cards and props to mime the preposition—no spoken words or noises allowed. Keep in mind that the preposition should be from Herman's point of view. If an actor makes a noise (as judged by the game monitor), the pair loses one point.

3. Guessers try to guess the preposition, using the word list for reference if needed. If a guesser correctly guesses the preposition, the actor flips over the card and puts it in a "words won" pile. The actor draws another word to act out. If the guesser is stuck, the actor can pass and pick another word.

4. After one minute, the game monitor says, "Switch!" Actors become guessers and vice versa, and the second half of the game begins. All unguessed words are out of play.

5. When time is up, the game monitor says, "Stop!" Teams score one point for each correctly guessed preposition. After the game monitor subtracts penalty points, the pair with the highest score wins.

Players:
Any number of pairs, plus a game monitor

Materials:
* Where's Herman? Character Cards
* Preposition Cards (cut apart and placed in a bag)
* Prepositions Word List
* Watch or timer
* Props

Where's Herman?
Preposition Cards

through	down	against
toward	on	aboard
under	in	around
over	inside	beyond
above	outside	between
below	off	behind
beside	within	across
by	with	past
next to	amid	throughout
near	among	along

Where's Herman?

Super Baby

Super Baby

Ms. Huff

Ms. Huff

Dr. Wells

Dr. Wells

Herman

Herman

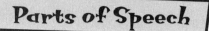
Word Buzz Review Game

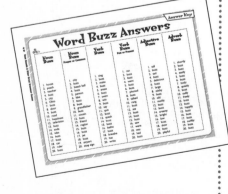

Skill:

Identifying parts of speech (review)

Players:

Any number from 1 to the entire class, plus a game monitor

Materials:

✳ Rules of the Game (page 47)

✳ Word Buzz Game Card (page 49)

✳ Answer Key (page 48)

✳ Timer

The Game in a Nutshell

In this grammar version of the number game Buzz, players read a list of words, substituting the word "buzz" for certain parts of speech.

Preparation

Choose the Word Buzz Game Card that corresponds to the part of speech that you want to review (nouns, verbs, adjectives, or adverbs). Make one copy of the Rules of the Game and Answer Key for the game monitor.

For a class or large-group exercise, copy the word list on the board, or display it on an overhead projector. For individual or small-group play, make one copy of the game card for each player.

Basic Grammar Skills

You can use "Word Buzz" either as a warm-up game or as a fast-paced review for previous grammar games about parts of speech. Before beginning, ask students to identify the target "buzz" words on the game card. Then play a practice round without a time limit for response.

Other Ways to Play

Random Word Buzz: Once students get the hang of the game, select readers randomly, rather than go in order around the class. Children won't be able to anticipate which word they will read and so must think on the spot to identify parts of speech.

Small-Group Version: Two or more players take turns reading the word list and saying "buzz" in place of key words. Each playing group needs one game monitor to check for errors.

Solitaire Version: One person completes the list as fast as possible. A game monitor times the person and checks for errors. The goal is for the player to improve his or her best time.

Spelling Buzz: Create a "Word Buzz" list of correctly and incorrectly spelled words; students must say "buzz" in place of the misspelled words.

Word Buzz

**Reading a list of words, substitute the word
"buzz" for certain parts of speech.**

How to Play:

1. Players read the word list and say "buzz" in place
of words that are certain parts of speech. For
example, in "Noun Buzz," players say "buzz" in
place of all words that are *not* nouns. The goal is
for the class to get through the entire list without
a mistake. If you have a list other than "Noun
Buzz," substitute your target part of speech for
nouns in these directions:

2. Going clockwise around a circle of players and
starting with the first word, each player in turn
reads the next word on the list. If the word is *not*
a noun, he or she must say "buzz" in place of the
word. The game monitor times each player and
uses the Answer Key to check for errors.

3. A "miss" happens when a player reads a non-noun
instead of saying "buzz," says "buzz" for a noun,
or takes more than 10 seconds. Each time a player
misses, he or she starts the game over by reading
the first word on the list, which is never a "buzz"
word. The next player reads the second word (or
says "buzz"), and so on.

4. Once students have mastered a list of words,
shorten the time period for response to three
seconds.

Players:

**Any number,
from 1 to the
entire class, plus
a game monitor**

Materials:

✶ Word Buzz
Game Card
(from your
teacher)
✶ Answer Key
✶ Timer

Word Buzz Answers

Noun Buzz	Noun Buzz — Proper or Common	Verb Buzz	Verb Buzz — Past or Present	Adjective Buzz	Adverb Buzz
1. house	1. city	1. sing	1. ran	1. tall	1. shortly
2. peach	2. buzz	2. buzz	2. buzz	2. buzz	2. buzz
3. teacher	3. beach ball	3. make	3. buzz	3. sad	3. buzz
4. buzz	4. buzz	4. buzz	4. went	4. buzz	4. easily
5. city	5. person	5. erase	5. buzz	5. delicious	5. buzz
6. Ohio	6. lake	6. buzz	6. buzz	6. buzz	6. buzz
7. buzz	7. buzz	7. swim	7. phoned	7. large	7. hotly
8. door	8. buzz	8. win	8. buzz	8. sticky	8. quietly
9. buzz	9. grandfather	9. buzz	9. talked	9. buzz	9. buzz
10. road	10. buzz	10. say	10. rang	10. old	10. sadly
11. happiness	11. cousin	11. quit	11. buzz	11. moldy	11. freely
12. television	12. buzz	12. buzz	12. ate	12. buzz	12. buzz
13. buzz	13. friend	13. speak	13. buzz	13. buzz	13. buzz
14. soda	14. region	14. buzz	14. buzz	14. creamy	14. happily
15. idea	15. buzz	15. buzz	15. buzz	15. bright	15. buzz
16. buzz	16. buzz	16. bathe	16. saw	16. low	16. buzz
17. buzz	17. jet	17. buzz	17. were	17. buzz	17. buzz
18. cat	18. buzz	18. breathe	18. was	18. slow	18. swiftly
19. ruler	19. airport	19. has	19. had	19. buzz	19. buzz
20. buzz	20. stop sign	20. write	20. buzz	20. playful	20. buzz

Word Buzz

Noun Buzz

Say "buzz" for each word that is NOT a noun.

1. house
2. peach
3. teacher
4. teach
5. city
6. Ohio
7. the
8. door
9. eat
10. road
11. happiness
12. television
13. big
14. soda
15. idea
16. strange
17. our
18. cat
19. ruler
20. done

Noun Buzz

Proper or Common

Say "buzz" for each word that is a PROPER noun.

1. city
2. Kansas City
3. beach ball
4. Samuel
5. person
6. lake
7. Lake Erie
8. Detroit Pistons
9. grandfather
10. Grandpa Jones
11. cousin
12. Gary
13. friend
14. region
15. Antarctica
16. Arctic
17. jet
18. Delta Airlines
19. airport
20. stop sign

Verb Buzz

Say "buzz" for each word that is NOT a verb.

1. sing
2. singer
3. make
4. gold
5. erase
6. happy
7. swim
8. win
9. winner
10. say
11. quit
12. quite
13. speak
14. quickly
15. bath
16. bathe
17. breath
18. breathe
19. has
20. write

Verb Buzz

Past or Present

Say "buzz" for each verb in the PRESENT TENSE.

1. ran
2. run
3. go
4. went
5. rings
6. phone
7. phoned
8. answer
9. talked
10. rang
11. create
12. ate
13. eats
14. watches
15. see
16. saw
17. were
18. was
19. had
20. ends

Adjective Buzz

Say "buzz" for each word that is NOT an adjective.

1. tall
2. give
3. sad
4. quickly
5. delicious
6. eat
7. large
8. sticky
9. carry
10. old
11. moldy
12. while
13. when
14. creamy
15. bright
16. low
17. slowly
18. slow
19. nearly
20. playful

Adverb Buzz

Say "buzz" for each word that is NOT an adverb.

1. shortly
2. play
3. tape
4. easily
5. red
6. quiet
7. hotly
8. quietly
9. happy
10. sadly
11. freely
12. grainy
13. silly
14. happily
15. young
16. wooded
17. speedy
18. swiftly
19. hilly
20. many

Pearls of Wisdom Auction

Players:

2 or more pairs

Materials:

* Rules of the Game (page 51)

* Pearls of Wisdom Quotations List (page 53)

* Empty egg carton for each pair

* Marker

* 25 "pearls" (beads, dried beans, pasta, or buttons) for each pair

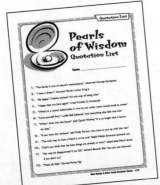

The Game in a Nutshell

Each pair of players has 25 "pearls" with which to bid on and purchase correctly punctuated quotations.

Preparation

Photocopy the Rules of the Game and Quotations List for each pair. Number the cups of each egg carton from 1 to 12 and provide each pair with 25 "pearls."

Basic Grammar Skills

Write the following sample sentences on the board. Have students practice and review how to place quotations marks and related punctuation in a sentence by correcting these examples:

Examples

They were hungry enough to eat a sawmill, wrote Ardyth Kennelly in *The Peaceable Kingdom*.

We are not amused! exclaimed Queen Victoria.

Invention arises directly from idleness", said Agatha Christie. possibly also from laziness—to save oneself trouble.

Corrections

"They were hungry enough to eat a sawmill," wrote Ardyth Kennelly in *The Peaceable Kingdom*.

"We are not amused!" exclaimed Queen Victoria.

"Invention arises directly from idleness," said Agatha Christie, "possibly also from laziness—to save oneself trouble."

Other Ways to Play

Everyday Pearls: Collect and use students' own grammar mistakes to create additional Pearls of Wisdom lists. The lists could emphasize other points of grammar such as commas, sentence fragments, and run-on sentences. They could also include spelling words.

Who's Who: Challenge children to earn bonus points by using references to identify all 12 speakers on the Pearls of Wisdom list.

Pearls of Wisdom

Bid on and purchase correctly punctuated quotations.

How to Play:

1. Read the 12 quotations on the list. Decide which ones are punctuated correctly.

2. Use your 25 pearls to bid on quotations that you believe are correct. To bid on a quotation, place any number of pearls in the egg-carton bin that matches the number of the quotation. You can place no pearls in a bin, or more pearls in one bin than another.

3. When time is up, no one can move or place another pearl. As a group, you will figure out which sentences are correct. For each correct sentence, the pair who bid the highest number of pearls wins a point. (If there's a tie, each top bidder wins a point.)

4. The pair that earns the most points wins the game.

Players:
2 or more pairs

Materials:
* Pearls of Wisdom Quotations List
* Empty egg carton
* 25 "pearls" (beads, dried beans, pasta, or buttons)

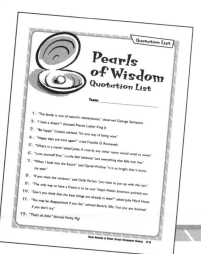

Quotation List

Pearls of Wisdom Quotation List

Team: _____

1. "The family is one of nature's masterpieces," observed George Santayana.
2. "I have a dream"! shouted Martin Luther King Jr.
3. "Be happy," Colette advised. "It's one way of being wise."
4. "Happy days are here again!" cried Franklin D. Roosevelt.
5. "What's in a name? asked Juliet. A rose by any other name would smell as sweet."
6. "Love yourself first," Lucille Ball believed, "and everything else falls into line."
7. "When I look into the future," said Oprah Winfrey "it is so bright that it burns my eyes."
8. "If you want the rainbow," said Dolly Parton, "you have to put up with the rain."
9. "The only way to have a friend is to be one" Ralph Waldo Emerson pointed out.
10. "Don't you think that the best things are already in view?" asked Julia Ward Howe.
11. "You may be disappointed if you fail," advised Beverly Sills, "but you are doomed if you don't try."
12. "That's all, folks" blurted Porky Pig!

Noun Hounds & Other Great Grammar Games 49

Pearls of Wisdom

**Below are the correctly punctuated sentences.
Asterisked (*) sentences are correct in the Quotations List.
Ideally, players will divide their pearls among bins 1, 4, 6, 8, 10,
and 11, and bid no pearls on the other sentences.**

* **1.** "The family is one of nature's masterpieces," observed George Santayana *(Spanish philosopher and writer)*.

  2. "I have a dream!" shouted Martin Luther King Jr. *(civil-rights leader)*

  3. "Be happy," Colette *(French writer)* advised. "It's one way of being wise."

* **4.** "Happy days are here again!" cried Franklin D. Roosevelt *(U.S. president)*.

  5. "What's in a name?" asked Juliet *(title character in Shakespeare's play* Romeo and Juliet*).* "A rose by any other name would smell as sweet."

* **6.** "Love yourself first," Lucille Ball *(actress)* believed, "and everything else falls into line."

  7. "When I look into the future," said Oprah Winfrey *(talk-show host)*, "it is so bright that it burns my eyes."

* **8.** "If you want the rainbow," said Dolly Parton *(country singer)*, "you have to put up with the rain."

  9. "The only way to have a friend is to be one," Ralph Waldo Emerson *(writer)* pointed out.

* **10.** "Don't you think that the best things are already in view?" asked Julia Ward Howe *(writer and creator of the* Battle Hymn of the Republic*).*

* **11.** "You may be disappointed if you fail," advised Beverly Sills *(opera singer)*, "but you are doomed if you don't try."

  12. "That's all, folks!" blurted Porky Pig *(cartoon character)*.

Pearls of Wisdom
Quotation List

Team: _____

1. "The family is one of nature's masterpieces," observed George Santayana.

2. "I have a dream"! shouted Martin Luther King Jr.

3. "Be happy," Colette advised, "It's one way of being wise."

4. "Happy days are here again!" cried Franklin D. Roosevelt.

5. "What's in a name? asked Juliet. A rose by any other name would smell as sweet."

6. "Love yourself first," Lucille Ball believed, "and everything else falls into line."

7. "When I look into the future" said Oprah Winfrey "it is so bright that it burns my eyes."

8. "If you want the rainbow," said Dolly Parton, "you have to put up with the rain."

9. "The only way to have a friend is to be one" Ralph Waldo Emerson pointed out.

10. "Don't you think that the best things are already in view?" asked Julia Ward Howe.

11. "You may be disappointed if you fail," advised Beverly Sills, "but you are doomed if you don't try."

12. "That's all, folks" blurted Porky Pig!

Compound Your Luck Game

Players:

2 to 6

Materials:

✻ Rules of the Game (game 55)

✻ Compound Your Luck (Mis)Fortunes (page 57)

✻ Spinner (page 56)

✻ Large envelope or shoe box

✻ Paper, pencil, and clipboard (for each player)

The Game in a Nutshell

Players change an unlucky fortune into a lucky one by using conjunctions.

Preparation

Photocopy one set of (Mis) Fortunes and cut them apart. Put the fortunes in an envelope or shoe box for random drawing. Photocopy the Rules of the Game for each player. Also, make one spinner per player (see page 56 for instructions).

Basic Grammar Skills

Conjunctions, such as *and, but, or,* and *yet*, link words in a sentence. Draw an unlucky fortune out of the bag. Have each student use a conjunction to turn the simple sentence into a compound sentence. Read aloud and compare sentences. Here are a few examples:

You will lose $100, *and* then you will find it again.

You will lose $100, *but* you will win the lottery the next day.

You will lose $100, *and yet* your best friend will find it.

Ask students: Where does the comma belong in a compound sentence? How many subjects are there? How does the meaning change if you change the conjunction in each sentence?

Other Ways to Play

Other Conjunctions: Replace conjunctions on the spinner with more complex ones, such as *because, since, unless, when, while, wherever,* and *whenever*.

Dashed Luck: In addition to commas, have students practice using dashes, colons, and semicolons to change their luck. Make a spinner that includes the punctuation marks: comma (,), semicolon (;), colon (:), dash (—), and period (.), and a "Word Change" space. If players spin a comma, they can use any conjunction to extend their fortune. If they spin a semicolon, colon, or dash, they use the punctuation mark alone to extend the fortune. As before, a period means that the bad fortune is final. "Word Change" allows players to add, subtract, or change any word in the fortune.

Your cat will lose all its hair.

Compound Your Luck

Be the first to cross the room by changing unlucky fortunes into lucky ones using conjunctions.

How to Play:

1. Line up on one side of the room facing the game monitor. The game monitor draws a (Mis)Fortune and reads it aloud. When the game monitor says, "Spin!" spin your spinners.

2. You have a limited time* to rewrite the (Mis)Fortune and change it to a lucky fortune using the conjunction that you've spun. If you spin a "period" (and so can't change your misfortune) you must stay in place and wait for the next (Mis)Fortune to try to advance.

3. When time is up, the game monitor will check your new fortune. If your fortune is correct, you can move one step forward. If your fortune is incorrect, you must stay in place.

4. The first player to advance eight steps across the room wins.

Players:
2 to 6

Materials:

✳ Compound Your Luck (Mis)Fortunes

✳ Spinner (for each player)

✳ Paper, pencil, and clipboard (for each player)

* Teacher: Set your own time limit, such as 30 or 60 seconds.

Compound Your Luck

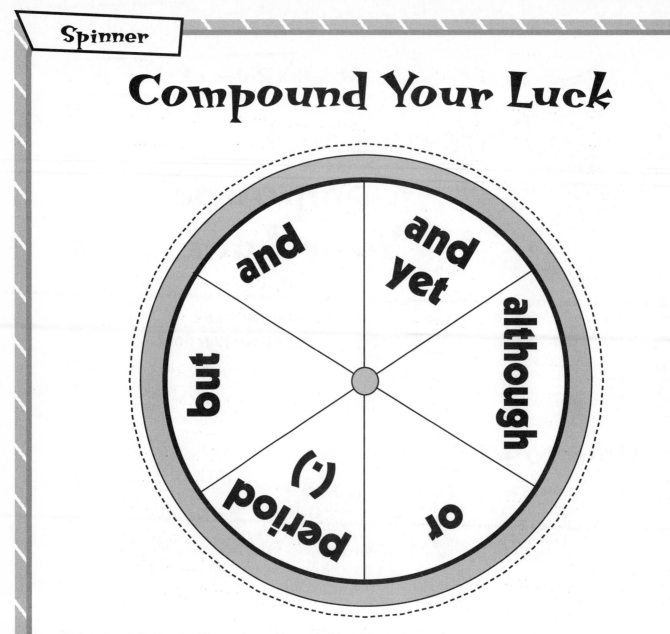

Assembling the Spinner

1. Cut out and mount a copy of the spinner pattern onto sturdy oak tag. Laminate the spinner and use a ballpoint pen to punch a small hole in the center.

2. To make a pointer, unbend one end of a large paper clip, as shown. Place the round end of the clip over the small hole. Insert a brass fastener through the hole and bend the two ends flat on the back side of the spinner to hold the paper clip in place.

3. Spin the paper clip. If the paper clip gets stuck, loosen the fastener. If the paper clip pops loose, tighten the fastener or use a larger one.

4. During game play, tell students that the paper clip must make at least two full rotations; otherwise, the player must spin again.

Your cat will lose all its hair.

Compound Your Luck (Mis)Fortunes

Your best friend will move to another city.	A bully will corner you on the playground.	A trip to the grocery store will seem to never end.
Your hair will turn purple and orange tomorrow.	The sun will melt your chocolate bar.	A mystery you are reading won't have the last page.
A large, black cat will cross your path.	An alarm clock will wake you up too early.	Your teacher will ask you to stay after school.
Rain will pour the next time you step outdoors.	You will get many cavities.	Your favorite television show will be cancelled.
A movie star will ignore you as he walks by.	A big hole will rip open in your clothing.	A comet will head straight for Earth.
Your friends will forget your birthday.	Your bike will get two flat tires.	You will find a worm in your bowl of ice cream.
You will get lost in a giant, boring mall.	Your science book will fall into enemy hands.	A bee will sting your arm more than once.
Your homework will fall down a sewer drain.	A secret admirer will remain secret.	A dog will chew up all of your socks.
A very, very long train will block your path.	A friend won't tell you a big secret.	Your team won't have enough players to play.
Your favorite store will close for good.	Your television will play only one channel.	You will lose a game of checkers to a young kid.
People will make fun of you for no reason.	Weeds will sprout on the floor of your classroom.	Your friends will plan a party without you.
Your chair will break as you sit in it.	A local rock band won't ask you to sing.	Your pet will run away from home.
Your lunch will get cold while you look for a seat.	A freak snow will fall on the last day of school.	A tornado will form near your town.

Run-On Riddle Relay Race

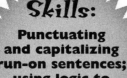

Skills:

Punctuating and capitalizing run-on sentences; using logic to solve riddles

Players:

2 teams of 3 to 5 students, plus a game monitor

Materials:

✳ Rules of the Game (page 59)

✳ Run-On Riddles and Answers (page 60)

✳ Word List (page 61)

✳ Different colored chalk or dry-erase markers

The Game in a Nutshell

Teams take turns correcting a run-on sentence that presents a riddle, then score bonus points by solving the riddle.

Preparation

Choose a riddle from the list and copy it on the board (listed from easier to harder). Encourage each team to choose a creative name, such as Rhyme Time or The E-racers. Provide each team with a different colored chalk or dry-erase marker and a copy of the Word List that corresponds to your chosen riddle. Have teams form two lines in front of the riddle on the board. Give the game monitor a copy of the Rules of the Game and the Riddles & Answer Key.

Basic Grammar Skills

A *run-on sentence* usually occurs when a writer combines two complete sentences into one, sometimes separated by a comma. These sentences should be separated by a period instead.

Riddles are rhymes or questions that often personify a mystery object. The following practice riddle, written as a run-on sentence, turns a storm cloud into a person:

> i fill up on water but i never drink then one by one
> my water drops sink

Work as a class to correct the riddle. Ask students: How many sentences are there? (*Two*) Where does one sentence end and the other begin? (*Hint: Find the two rhyming words, which usually come at the end of sentence.*) Besides adding a period, what else do you change when you end one sentence and start another? (*Capitalize the first letter of the new sentence.*) There are three commas missing. Where do they go? The corrected riddle reads:

> I fill up on water, but I never drink.
> Then, one by one, my water drops sink.

Other Ways to Play

Cooperative Riddlers: Form one line in front of the riddle and challenge students to correct it as fast as they can with each student making one correction in turn. Record the finished time. Then challenge students to beat this time on the next riddle challenge.

Tough Riddlers: For children who are good at solving riddles, omit the word list and challenge teams to solve the riddle without it. Award five bonus points for a correct guess.

Run-On Riddle Relay

Correct a run-on sentence that presents a riddle, then score bonus points by solving the riddle.

How to Play:

1. The game monitor will write a riddle on the board, then says, "Run-on!" At the command, the first member of Team 1 goes to the board and makes *one* change. He or she could add a punctuation mark, for example. This player hands the chalk or marker to the next teammate and goes to the back of the line.

2. The first member of Team 2 then takes a turn. He or she makes one change, such as turning a lower-case letter into a capital letter. This player then hands the chalk or marker to the next teammate and goes to the back of the line.

3. A player can use a turn to correct a teammate's mistake or a mistake made by the other team. If a player can't find a mistake, he or she can pass and lose the turn.

4. Teams take turns making corrections until the game monitor sees that the riddle is correctly punctuated and capitalized, and says, "Run no more!"

5. Teams score one point for each correction, as shown by the different colors of chalk or marker. Each team has 30 seconds to circle a word on the Word List that best solves the riddle. A correct guess counts for two bonus points. The team with the higher total score wins.

Players:

2 teams of 3 to 5 students, plus a game monitor

Materials:

* Different colored chalk or dry-erase marker for each team
* Word List

Run-On Riddles & Answers

Choose a riddle (listed from easy to challenging) and write it on the board. Teams will take turns correcting the run-on sentence and guessing the answer.

Riddle 1

i get wetter and wetter each time i dry as much as i drip i can never cry

Answer:

I get wetter and wetter each time I dry. As much as I drip, I can never cry. *(Towel)*

Riddle 2

i have many stories but i'm not a skyscraper the cart comes before the horse when it is on paper

Answer:

I have many stories, but I'm not a skyscraper. The cart comes before the horse when it is on paper. *(Library; "cart" comes before "horse" alphabetically.)*

Riddle 3

i am often seen on water but i never get wet i am often seen on glass but i haven't broken yet

Answer:

I am often seen on water, but I never get wet. I am often seen on glass, but I haven't broken yet. *(Reflection)*

Riddle 4

the more you take away the longer i stray don't take too much without leaving me a crutch

Answer:

The more you take away, the longer I stray. Don't take too much without leaving me a crutch. *(Tunnel)*

Riddle 5

the longer i stand the shorter i am the brighter i glow the faster i go

Answer:

The longer I stand, the shorter I am. The brighter I glow, the faster I go. *(Candle)*

Riddle 6 (Challenge)

i was going to study in school i met a clown and a fool the fool had seven cats the clown had seven bats how many of us in all were on our way to study hall

Answer:

I was going to study in school. I met a clown and a fool. The fool had seven cats. The clown had seven bats. How many of us in all were on our way to study hall? *(One—the speaker)*

Run-On Riddles

Team One

Riddle 1

WORD LIST: beach, dish, rain cloud, towel, steam iron, puddle, umbrella, raincoat, sprinkler, onion

Riddle 2

WORD LIST: building, skyscraper, library, dictionary, apartment, buggy, street, road, alley, book

Riddle 3

WORD LIST: wave, ripple, boat, fingerprint, lily pad, reflection, shadow, sign, sunset, photograph

Riddle 4

WORD LIST: road, hiker, dog leash, subtraction, rope, footstep, snake, tunnel, river, hallway

Riddle 5

WORD LIST: sand castle, mountain, shadow, rocket, streetlight, candle, sun, firefly, glowworm, flashlight

Riddle 6 (Challenge)

WORD LIST: one, three, seven, fourteen, seventeen, forty-nine

Team Two

Riddle 1

WORD LIST: beach, dish, rain cloud, towel, steam iron, puddle, umbrella, raincoat, sprinkler, onion

Riddle 2

WORD LIST: building, skyscraper, library, dictionary, apartment, buggy, street, road, alley, book

Riddle 3

WORD LIST: wave, ripple, boat, fingerprint, lily pad, reflection, shadow, sign, sunset, photograph

Riddle 4

WORD LIST: road, hiker, dog leash, subtraction, rope, footstep, snake, tunnel, river, hallway

Riddle 5

WORD LIST: sand castle, mountain, shadow, rocket, streetlight, candle, sun, firefly, glowworm, flashlight

Riddle 6 (Challenge)

WORD LIST: one, three, seven, fourteen, seventeen, forty-nine

The Write Rules
Sentence Review

Skill:

Correcting punctuation and other grammar errors in sentences

Players:

Any number, from 1 to the whole class, plus a game monitor

Materials:

* Rules of the Game (page 63)

* The Write Rules (pages 65–66)

* Pencil

The Game in a Nutshell

Players correct a grammatically incorrect list of rules.

Preparation

Photocopy the Rules of the Game for each player or team. Choose either The Write Rules 1 (easier) or The Write Rules 2 (harder) and make one copy per player or team.

For team play, have each group take on the last name of a favorite author (Paulsen, Blume, Cleary) and assign roles:

* editor-in-chief (to read copy aloud and lead the group)
* researcher (to look up words in the dictionary)
* copy editor (to record corrections)

Basic Grammar Skills

The Write Rules 1 emphasizes contractions, spelling, and end-of-sentence punctuation. The Write Rules 2 provides practice in using a variety of punctuation marks, fixing run-on and fragmented sentences, eliminating wordiness, avoiding double negatives, checking for agreement, and proofreading for mistakes.

Other Ways to Play

Deluxe Rules: Have students add their own rules to the list. One strategy is to add new rules based on writing mistakes students make.

Style-Wise: As a class, create a list of rules to improve writing style. Here are a few items to start your list:

* Clichés are old hat. Don't use them to death.
* Replace common words with words that are more or less specific.
* Repeating yourself is like saying the same thing twice or over and over again.
* The passive voice is to be turned into the active voice.
* Don't overuse lively, interesting, descriptive adjectives.

The Write Rules

Correct a grammatically incorrect list of rules.

How to Play:

1. The game monitor will give you a copy of The Write Rules facedown.

2. When the game monitor says, "The proof is in the writing," flip over your paper and begin correcting errors. When time is up, stop writing.

3. The game monitor will help correct the sentences. You earn one point for each correction. The player or team with the most points wins.

Players:

Any number, from 1 to the whole class, plus a game monitor

Materials:

✳ The Write Rules

✳ Pencil

The Write Rules

The Write Rules 1

1. There's one tiny thing missing from this sentence.

2. It's easy to overlook tiny things.

3. You're on the right track.

4. One dot is all that this sentence needs.

5. How can we ask such an easy question?

6. Don't worry if you goof up.

7. Be happy that you can repair errors.

8. Don't read this aloud. You can't hear what's wrong.

9. Three spelling mistakes in one sentence is three too many.

10. Are you done? Stop!

The Write Rules 2

1. You better end every sentence with punctuation—or else!

2. If I were you, I would delete commas that you don't need.

3. If a comma is missing, the reader might run out of breath and die.

4. Run-on sentences are ugly. They make you sound hyper.

5. Be brief! Cut out extra words.

6. "Put punctuation in its place," I say.

7. Don't use double negatives. Understand?

8. Avoid sentence fragments.

9. A subject, verb, and pronoun have to agree with each other. Don't you agree?

10. Proofread your writing carefully to get rid of all mistakes.

Name: _____

The Write Rules 1

Each sentence contains at least one error.
How many errors can you find and correct?

1. Theres one tiny thing missing from this sentence.

2. Its easy to overlook tiny things.

3. Your on the right track.

4. One dot is all that this sentence needs

5. How can we ask such an easy question

6. Dont worry if you goof up.

7. be happy that you can repare errors.

8. Dont read this allowed. You can't here whats wrong.

9. Three speling misteaks in one sentence is three to many.

10. Are you done? Stop

Name: _____

The Write Rules 2

**Each sentence contains at least one error.
How many errors can you find and correct?**

1. You better end every sentence with punctuation—or else

2. If I were you, I would delete commas, that you don't, need.

3. If a comma is missing the reader might run out of breath and die.

4. Run-on sentences are ugly they make you sound hyper.

5. Be brief! Cut out and eliminate extra, additional words that you don't need.

6. "Put punctuation in its place", I say."

7. Don't use no double negatives. Understand?

8. No sentence fragments.

9. A subject, verb, and pronoun has to agree with themselves. Don't you agrees?

10. Proofread you're writing carefuly to rid of all misteaks.

Crack Me Up! Capitalization Challenge

Skills:

Proofreading a text for capitalization mistakes; using grammar and language skills to decode messages

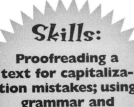

Players:

Any number of individuals or pairs

Materials:

* Rules of the Game (page 68)
* Crack Me Up! Jokes (pages 70–71)
* Pencils

The Game in a Nutshell

Players decode the punch lines of jokes by correcting capitalization errors in a letter or invitation.

Preparation

Choose one of the texts on pages 70–71 and photocopy one for each player or pair. Photocopy the Rules of the Game for each player.

Basic Grammar Skills

Ask students: What types of words are capitalized? Review the categories below and ask students to provide an example of each one:

- Words at the beginning of a sentence
- Names of groups and organizations (the International Red Cross)
- Titles of books, movies, songs, etc. (*The Guinness Book of Records*)
- Names of months or days of the week (October, Tuesday)
- Names of people, including titles (Grandma Moses, but not grandmas in general)
- Geographic names, such as cities and states (Pasadena, California; the Wild West).

Other Ways to Play

Grammar Spies: Have students create their own secret messages using the "Crack Me Up!" grammar code.

Spelling Spies: Make coded messages that contain spelling mistakes instead of capitalization errors. The first letters of each misspelled word spell out a secret message.

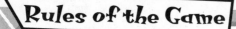

Crack Me Up!

Correct capitalization errors to decode the punch lines of jokes.

How to Play:

1. Your teacher will give you a passage to correct.

2. Correct all the capitalization errors in the passage. The incorrect letters that you fix spell the punch line of a joke. If the letters don't spell the punch line, you made a mistake.

Players:
Any number of individuals or pairs

Materials:

✳ Crack Me Up! Joke

✳ Pencil

Crack Me Up! Jokes

1.

Dear Grandma,

I know, **G**randma, that you love nature. I just joined the **U**nited **A**nimals and **N**ature **A**ssociation. **C**an you join, too? We meet every **O**ctober and **M**ay in the city of **E**vanston, **I**llinois.

Love,
Nate

Punch line: Iguana come in.

....

2.

Anita **W**anita invites you to her **e**leventh birthday party!

Time: 12:00 noon
Place: Anita's **b**ackyard
Day: Tuesday
Please bring **a** **n**ew **k**ite and an **e**ar of corn.
Thank you.

Punch line: A wet blanket

....

3.

Dear Mother Ship,

I have landed on the planet called Earth. The people of Earth have **t**wo **f**eet and no lasers in their **e**yes. How strange!

This summer, I will travel **w**est to the **s**tates of South Dakota and **O**regon. In September, I will visit another western region. Perhaps the Great Salt **L**ake of Utah will be home to intelligent beings.

Sincerely,
Otto the Alien

Punch line: It flew solo (so low).

4.

April 1, 2050

President Metalhead
Nuts and Volts **C**orporation
001 Computer **L**ane **E**ast
Steeltown, **O**hio 01011

Dear **P**resident Metalhead:

I bought your **a**luminum machine called **T**ippy the **R**obot in **A**tlanta, Georgia. Mr. President, **T**ippy tips over.

I gave Tippy a book called *The Easy, Quick User's Guide to Everything, Everyone, and Nothing*. It didn't help.

Next, Tippy joined a group called the **O**rder of **F**raternal **D**onkeys. This **e**xcellent **n**ational group tried to teach Tippy how to stand up. **I**nstead, Tippy taught them how to fall.

I would like to return Tippy to your **a**ddress. However, Tippy's box keeps tipping over, too. What can I do?

Sincerely,

Sue U. Knot, Attorney-at-**L**aw

Punch line: Cleopatra, the Queen of Denial (the Nile)

1. Crack Me Up!

Directions: Read the letter below. Find and circle all the lowercase letters that should be capitals. The circled letters will spell the punch line of the joke at the bottom.

Dear Grandma,

i know, grandma, that you love nature. I just joined the united animals and nature association. can you join, too? We meet every october and may in the city of evanston, illinois.

Love,
nate

Knock, knock. Who's there? Iguana. Iguana who?

__ __ __ __ __   __ __ __ __

2. Crack Me Up!

Directions: Circle all lowercase letters that should be capitals and capitals that should be lowercase. The letters spell the punch line of the joke at the bottom.

anita wanita invites you to her Eleventh birthday party!

time: 12:00 noon

Place: Anita's Backyard

Day: Tuesday

PLease bring A New Kite and an Ear of corn.

thank you.

What do you get when you cross a boring sheep and a bucket of water?

__ __ __   __ __ __ __

(Hint: What do you call someone who takes all the fun out of a party?)

4. Crack Me Up!

Directions: Circle all lowercase letters that should be capitals and capitals that should be lowercase. The letters spell the punch line of the joke at the bottom.

April 1, 2050
President Metalhead
Nuts and Volts corporation
001 Computer lane east
Steeltown, ohio 01011

Dear president Metalhead:

I bought your Aluminum machine called tippy the robot in atlanta, Georgia. Mr. President, Tippy tips over. I gave Tippy a book called *THe Easy, quick user's Guide to everything, everyone, and nothing.* It didn't help. Next, Tippy joined a group called the order of fraternal donkeys. This Excellent National group tried to teach Tippy how to stand up. instead, Tippy taught them how to fall. I would like to return Tippy to your Address. However, Tippy's box keeps tipping over, too. What can I do?

Sincerely,
Sue U. Knot, Attorney-at-law

What famous ruler answered every question, "No!"?

_ _ _ _ _ _ _ _ _ , _ _ _ _ _ _

(Hint: The last word sounds like what famous river?)

3. Crack Me Up!

Directions: Circle all lowercase letters that should be capitals and capitals that should be lowercase. The letters spell the punch line of the joke at the bottom.

Dear Mother Ship,

i have landed on the planet called Earth. The people of Earth have Two Feet and no Lasers in their Eyes. How strange!

This summer, I will travel West to the States of South Dakota and oregon. In September, I will visit another western region. Perhaps the Great Salt lake of Utah will be home to intelligent beings.

Sincerely,
otto the Alien

Why did the lone duck crash into a tree?

_ _ _ _ _ _ _ _ _ _ _ _

(Hint: The last word sounds like two words.)

Word Jam Concentration

Skill:

Combining words to form common contractions

Players:

An even number, from 8 to about 20, plus a game monitor

Materials:

* Rules of the Game (page 73)

* Word Jam Card Set (page 76)

* Word Jam Turn Signal Cards (page 75)

* Answer Key (page 74)

The Game in a Nutshell

In a variation of Concentration, players find and combine two words to form contractions.

Preparation

Photocopy the Word Jam Card Set onto opaque paper. You'll need two to four cards per player; if you have a large group, make duplicate word pairs. Photocopy and cut out the Word Jam Turn Signals along the dotted lines, and give one card to each player. Have students fold their cards in half so that the words face out.

Make a copy of the Answer Key for the game monitor. You may also want to make an overhead transparency of the Rules of the Game.

Before starting, arrange players' desks in a grid. Have each player set his or her Turn Signal so that the "I'm Ready to Jam!" side is in clear view.

Basic Grammar Skills

When you combine two words into one by omitting one or more letters, you form a *contraction*. An apostrophe takes the place of the omitted letters.

Other Ways to Play

Advanced Contractions: Add cards for the subject pronouns *what, there,* and *who.* Here are some sample contractions for *there:* *there's, there'll, there've, there'd.*

Two-Player Game: Use the cards to play a regular Concentration game. Set out all the cards facedown in a large grid. Players take turns flipping over any two cards. If players can form a contraction, they write it on paper, remove the cards from the grid, and take another turn. If they can't form a contraction, they flip the cards facedown again and end the turn. Check the list of contractions at the end of the game and cross out erroneous ones before scoring one point per contraction.

Word Jam

In this variation of Concentration, find and combine two words to form contractions.

How to Play:

Players:

An even number, from 8 to about 20, plus a game monitor

1. The game monitor will deal one card facedown to each player. Read your card silently but keep the word hidden.

2. When it's your turn, stand up and read the word (or words) on your card aloud.

3. Choose a player whose Turn Signal says "I'm Ready to Jam!" This player reads his or her word aloud.

4. Can you form a contraction out of the two words?
    YES: Write the contraction on the board for the game monitor to check.
    NO: Your turn is over. Skip to step 6.
(If a card has two words, you can use either word. A Wild Card can be any word that you choose.)

Materials:

❋ Word Jam Card Set

❋ Word Jam Turn Signal Cards

5. If your contraction is correct, you earn both word cards. The game monitor will hand you and the other player a new card.

6. Flip over your Turn Signal so that it reads, "I Just Jammed!" The player who read the second word takes the next turn.

7. After everyone has taken a first turn, all Turn Signals should read, "I Just Jammed!" To begin the second round, all players flip their Turn Signals to read, "I'm Ready to Jam!"

8. The game continues until all cards are gone. Score two points for each word pair. The player with the highest score wins.

Word Jam Contractions List

Word Jam provides practice in forming the following contractions:

I will: I'll
you will: you'll
he will: he'll
she will: she'll
it will: it'll
we will: we'll
they will: they'll

I would: I'd
you would: you'd
he would: he'd
she would: she'd
it would: it'd
we would: we'd
they would: they'd

I am: I'm
you are: you're
he is: he's
she is: she's
it is: it's
we are: we're
they are: they're

I have: I've
you have: you've
he has: he's
she has: she's
it has: it's
we have: we've
they have: they've

I had: I'd
you had: you'd
he had: he'd
she had: she'd
it had: it'd
we had: we'd
they had: they'd

would have: would've
could have: could've
should have: should've

is not: isn't
are not: aren't
was not: wasn't
were not: weren't
has not: hasn't
have not: haven't
had not: hadn't
do not: don't
does not: doesn't
did not: didn't
cannot: can't
will not: won't
would not: wouldn't
could not: couldn't
should not: shouldn't

Word Jam Turn Signals

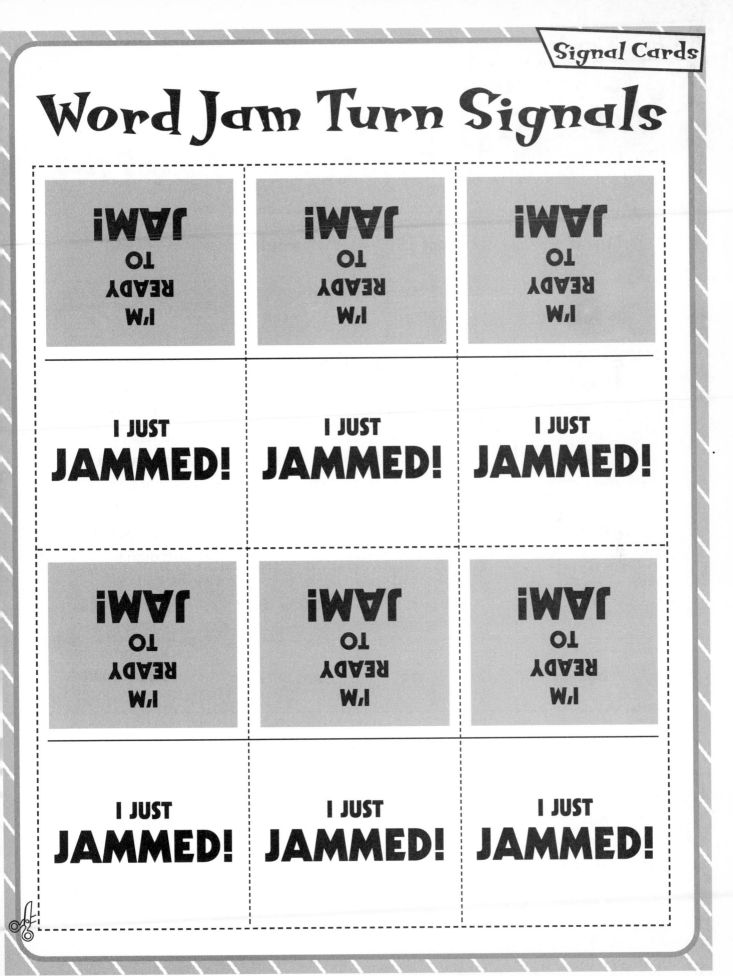

I'M READY TO **JAM!**

I'M READY TO **JAM!**

I'M READY TO **JAM!**

I JUST **JAMMED!**

I JUST **JAMMED!**

I JUST **JAMMED!**

I'M READY TO **JAM!**

I'M READY TO **JAM!**

I'M READY TO **JAM!**

I JUST **JAMMED!**

I JUST **JAMMED!**

I JUST **JAMMED!**

Word Jam Card Set

I or it	not	would	will
he or she	not	can	am or is
we	not	can	will
you	not	had	could
they	not	did	not
not	am or is	do or does	WILD CARD!
not	am or are	was or were	WILD CARD!
not	am or are	have or has	WILD CARD!
not	should	have or has	WILD CARD!

Cooking Up Plurals Game

Skills:

Pluralizing regular and irregular nouns; looking up words in a dictionary; creative writing

Players:

2 to 4

Materials:

* Rules of the Game (page 78)

* Cooking Up Plurals game board and playing pieces (page 80)

* Recipe for Disaster (page 79)

* Dictionary

* Coin or other small object

* Pencil

The Game in a Nutshell

Players race from Start to a ghoulish Finish by pluralizing the ingredients in a delightfully disgusting recipe.

Preparation

Photocopy the Rules of the Game and recipe for each player. Make an enlarged copy of the game board. Cut out the playing pieces along the dotted lines, then fold along the solid lines so pieces can stand on their own. Provide the playing group with a dictionary to verify challenges and look up irregular plurals.

Basic Grammar Skills

To pluralize most nouns, just add an *s: boat* becomes *boats.* Of course, some nouns can throw students off track. Review ways to make these types of nouns plural:

● gravy (change *y* to *ies*)
● dish (add *es*)
● thief (change *f* to *ves*)
● cactus (change *us* to *i* or add *es*—either is correct in many cases)
● alga (add *e*)
● foot (change the spelling, in this case to *feet*)

Look up nouns with irregular plurals in the dictionary. Then look up the word *recipe* and ask students: Why doesn't the dictionary list a plural form for this noun? If students aren't sure, look up a few more words, such as *paper, pen,* and *group,* until students realize that the dictionary does not list regular plurals.

Other Way to Play

Recipe Writing: Provide students with a list of irregular plurals and ask them to concoct their own ghoulish or silly recipes. They will need to change the plurals into singular form, following the format of the Recipe for Disaster.

Cooking Up Plurals

Race from START to a ghoulish FINISH by pluralizing the ingredients in a delightfully disgusting recipe.

How to Play:

1. Place all the playing pieces at START.

2. To determine how many spaces you will move, the player to your left hides a coin in either hand. Guess which fist holds the coin:

- If you guess correctly, move two spaces.
- If you guess incorrectly, move one space.

3. Here's what to do if you land on one of the following spaces on the board:

Double Disaster: Change one word in the ingredient list to a plural. For example, change *1 eye* to *2 eyes*.

Beef It Up: Add a plural word to the end of the ingredient list.

Hit the Dictionary: Find an irregular plural in the dictionary. Read the plural spelling aloud.

4. After you take a turn, another player can challenge your answer:

- If the challenger is correct, you must move back one space and end your turn.
- If you are correct, move forward one space and end the turn.
- If no one challenges your answer, stay put and end your turn.

5. The first player to reach FINISH wins.

Players:
2 to 4

Materials:

* Cooking Up Plurals game board and playing pieces
* Recipe for Disaster
* Dictionary
* Coin or other small object
* Pencil

Name: _____

Recipe for Disaster

Double this recipe for twice the yucky fun! Follow the game instructions to make the single ingredients plural and to add your own ingredients to the end of the list.

Ingredients

1 eye of newt	2 eyes of _____
1 leaf of dandelion	2 _____ of _____
1 wing of wasp	2 _____ of _____
1 beak of octopus	2 _____ of _____
1 tooth of hippopotamus	2 _____ of _____
1 dash of hot pepper	2 _____ of _____
1 loaf of stale bread	2 _____ of _____
1 toe of mouse	2 _____ of _____
1 skin of cranberry	2 _____ of _____
1 antenna of fly	2 _____ of _____
1 anchovy	2 _____
2 _____	
2 _____	
2 _____	
2 _____	
2 _____	
2 _____	

Cooking Up Plurals

Race from START to a ghoulish FINISH by pluralizing the ingredients in a delightfully disgusting recipe.

START

Beef It Up!

Double Disaster

Take another turn.

Hit the Dictionary

Beef It Up!

Hit the Dictionary

Double Disaster

Beef It Up!

Take another turn.

Hit the Dictionary

Double Disaster

Double Disaster

Lose a turn.

Hit the Dictionary

Beef It Up!

Double Disaster

Lose a turn.

Double Disaster

Beef It Up!

Double Disaster

FINISH

Playing Pieces

Sammy Supreme

Ghoulia Child

P.U. Pierre

The Goofy Gormay

Sound Sisters Board Game

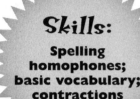

Skills:

Spelling homophones; basic vocabulary; contractions

Players:

2 to 4

Materials:

* Rules of the Game (page 82)
* Sound Sisters game board and playing pieces (page 84)
* Sound Sisters Cards (page 85)
* Coin or other small object
* Dictionary

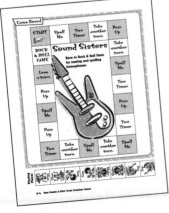

The Game in a Nutshell

Players are rock stars racing to Rock & Roll Fame by naming and spelling "Sound Sisters," or homophones.

Preparation

Make an enlarged photocopy of the Sound Sisters game board and cards. Cut apart the cards and the playing pieces along the dotted lines. Fold the playing pieces along the solid lines so pieces can stand on their own. Photocopy the Rules of the Game for each player. Players will need a coin or other object for advancing around the board and a dictionary for verifying "Two Timer" definitions.

Basic Grammar Skills

Homophones (from the Greek word for "same voice") are two or more words that sound the same but have different meanings. They may have the same spelling—*general* can mean either "military leader" or "not specific." Or they may have different meanings—*beat* and *beet* are homophones that refer to "rhythm" and a "red vegetable," respectively. Some homophones are words that can be either nouns or verbs: *file* can be a noun that means "report folder" or a verb that means "to store." Contractions such as *they're, it's,* and *you're* are a common source of confusion with homophone partners such as *their* or *there, its,* and *your.* (See "Word Jam Concentration, page 72, for practice in spelling contractions.)

Other Ways to Play

More Homophones: Challenge children to add cards to the game. They'll find homophones in books about spelling or vocabulary, in rhyming dictionaries, and in everyday usage.

Sound Sister Lyrics: Choose a popular song such as *Row, Row, Row Your Boat* and have children write homophone lyrics to the tune:

Grow, grow, grow your food,
Quickly sprouts a beet.
Higher, higher, higher, higher,
Beets just can't be beat.

Sound Sisters

**Race to Rock & Roll Fame
by naming and spelling homophones.**

How to Play:

1. Place all game pieces on START. Shuffle the cards and place them facedown next to the game board.

2. Players take turns. To determine how many spaces you will move, the player to your left hides a coin in either hand. Guess which fist holds the coin:

- If you guess correctly, move two spaces.
- If you guess incorrectly, move one space.

3. If you land on Pair Up, Spell Me, or Two Timer, the person on your left draws the top card and becomes a reader. Here's what to do next:

- **Pair Up:** The reader reads and spells the word after "Pair Up." If you can spell a homophone of the word, stay in place. If you can spell two homophones, take another turn. (The answer is in the "Spell Me" section of the card.)

- **Spell Me:** The reader chooses one of the homophones listed after "Spell Me." He or she reads the word and its definition. Based on the definition, you spell the homophone aloud. If you are correct, stay in place.

- **Two Timer:** The reader reads and spells the word after "Two Timer." If you can give two meanings for the word, stay in place. If you can give three meanings, take another turn.

4. If you answer incorrectly, go back one space and end your turn. Ignore the instructions on that space. The reader puts the card on the bottom of the deck.

5. The first player to reach Rock & Roll Fame wins.

Players:

2 to 4

Materials:

✻ Sound Sisters game board and playing pieces

✻ Sound Sisters Cards

✻ Coin or other small object

✻ Dictionary

Sound Sisters Cards

Pair Up: Brake

Spell Me (pick one):
  Brake: Stop a bike
  Break: Short rest

Two Timer: Well

Pair Up: Here

Spell Me (pick one):
  Here: This place
  Hear: Listen to

Two Timer: Bear

Pair Up: Coarse

Spell Me (pick one):
  Coarse: Rough
  Course: Class

Two Timer: Pick

Pair Up: Poll

Spell Me (pick one):
  Poll: Ask an opinion
  Pole: Long stick

Two Timer: Bowl

Pair Up: There

Spell Me (pick one):
  There: That place
  Their: Owned by
    them
  They're: They are

Two Timer: Part

Pair Up: Too

Spell Me (pick one):
  Too: Also
  Two: 1 + 1
  To: "To be or not to
    be"

Two Timer: Ruler

Pair Up: Meat

Spell Me (pick one):
  Meat: Food
  Meet: Get to know
  Mete: Give out

Two Timer: Chicken

Pair Up: Its

Spell Me (pick one):
  Its: Belonging to it
  It's: Short for "it is"

Two Timer: Creep

Pair Up: Reign

Spell Me (pick one):
  Rain: Wet weather
  Reign: Rule
  Rein: Strap for horses

Two Timer: Track

Pair Up: Heir

Spell Me (pick one):
  Heir: A prince, for
    example
  Air: What you
    breathe

Two Timer: Bat

Pair Up: Shoo

Spell Me (pick one):
  Shoo: Scram
  Shoe: Footwear

Two Timer: Chip

Pair Up: Stake

Spell Me (pick one):
  Stake: Pole or stick
  Steak: Meaty dinner

Two Timer: File

Pair Up: Gail

Spell Me (pick one):
  Gail: Girl's name
  Gale: Storm

Two Timer: Park

Pair Up: Beet

Spell Me (pick one):
  Beet: Red vegetable
  Beat: Defeat

Two Timer: Fit

Pair Up: Ware

Spell Me (pick one):
  Wear: Put on
  Ware: Item for sale
  Where: What place?

Two Timer: Arm

Pair Up:

Spell Me (pick one):

Two Timer:

Pair Up: Pair

Spell Me (pick one):
  Pear: Yellow fruit
  Pare: Peel a fruit
  Pair: Couple

Two Timer: Press

Pair Up: Foul

Spell Me (pick one):
  Foul: Not fair
  Fowl: Dinner bird

Two Timer: Fair

Pair Up: Scene

Spell Me (pick one):
  Scene: Setting
  Seen: Spotted

Two Timer: Bill

Pair Up:

Spell Me (pick one):

Two Timer:

Game Board

| START | Spell Me | Two Timer | Take another turn. | Pair Up |

Sound Sisters

Race to Rock & Roll Fame by naming and spelling homophones.

ROCK & ROLL FAME

Take another turn.

Spell Me

Lose a turn.

Two Timer

Pair Up

Pair Up

Spell Me

Two Timer

Pair Up

Two Timer

Two Timer | Take another turn. | Spell Me | Take another turn. | Spell Me

Playing Pieces

Elvin · Elvin · Gem · Gem · Sheba · Sheba · Zap · Zap

Seven-Up Spelling Review

Skills:
Recognizing and correcting misspelled words; using a dictionary

Players:
2

Materials:
✶ Rules of the Game (page 86)

✶ Seven-Up Spelling Cards (pages 87– 88)

✶ Dictionary

✶ Pencils

The Game in a Nutshell
Players take turns correcting misspelled words with the goal of turning all seven cards either Triceratops-side up or Tyrannosaurus-side up.

Preparation
Photocopy the Rules of the Game for each player. Make a double-sided photocopy of the Seven-Up Spelling Cards onto oak tag. The spelling words on the front of each card should correspond to the spelling words on the back. Cut apart the cards and choose seven cards that match players' ability. Set aside blank cards and extra cards for later games. Students will need a dictionary to verify challenges, and pencils with erasers. Have students look up and memorize the spelling of *Tyrannosaurus* and *Triceratops* before playing the game.

Basic Grammar Skills
The spelling words in "Seven-Up Spelling" include some of the most common mistakes people make, including:
- the "*i* before *e* except after *c*" rule (*piece*) and exceptions to this rule (*height*)
- double consonants (*across* not *accross*)
- tricky vowels (*separate* not *seperate*)
- silent letters (*February* not *Febuary*)
- one word versus two words (*a lot* not *alot*)
- contractions (*didn't* not *did'nt*)
- tricky verbs (*cried* not *cryed*)

Other Ways to Play
Simpler Version: Play with five cards instead of seven. Choose or make cards with easier spelling words.

New Spelling Words: Fill in your own tricky spelling words on the cards. To avoid confusion, make sure that the misspelled version is not another legitimate word (e.g., *lets* and *let's* are both correct) or cannot be turned into another legitimate word (e.g., *quiet* could be *quiet* or *quite*). Each card should have two or three misspelled words.

Seven-Up Spelling

Take turns correcting misspelled words to turn all seven cards either Triceratops-side up or Tyrannosaurus-side up.

How to Play:

1. Choose a dinosaur, either Triceratops or Tyrannosaurus. Line up all seven cards so that alternating dinosaurs are faceup, starting with a Triceratops card.

2. The Tyrannosaurus player takes the first turn by looking for a misspelled word on a Triceratops card and writing the correct spelling next to it. When the player puts down the pencil, the word becomes "official" and can't be changed.

3. The Triceratops player looks up the word in the dictionary:
- If the Tyrannosaurus player's spelling is correct, flip over the card so that it is Tyrannosaurus-side up.
- If the spelling is incorrect, the Triceratops player erases the word; the card remains Triceratops-side up.

The Triceratops player takes a turn, looking for a misspelled word on a Tyrannosaurus card.

4. Players can pass on any turn—for example, when an opponent's faceup cards have no more spelling mistakes. After three passes in a row, the player with more cards faceup must spell his or her dinosaur's name from memory to win. If the player can't spell it, the game is a tie.

5. A dinosaur becomes "extinct" when the other dinosaur is faceup on all seven cards. The player who's still alive must correctly spell the name of his or her dinosaur to win. Otherwise, the other player can turn over any three cards and play continues.

Players:
2

Materials:
* 7 Seven-Up Spelling Cards
* Dictionary
* Pencils

Tyrannosaurus

Triceratops

Seven-Up Spelling Cards

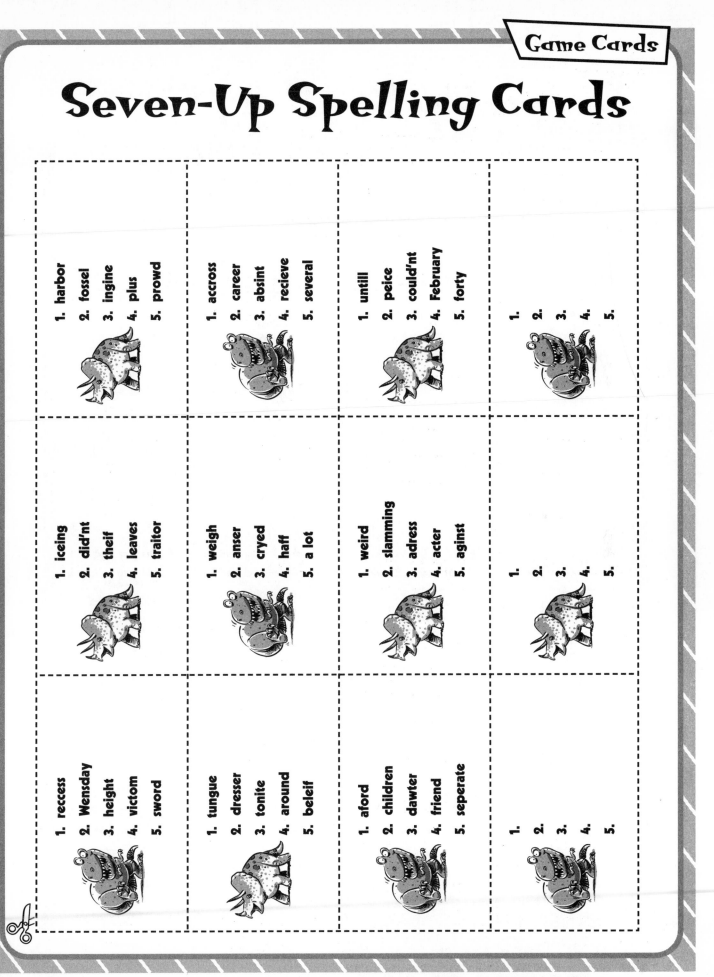

1. harbor
2. fossel
3. ingine
4. plus
5. prowd

1. accross
2. career
3. absint
4. recieve
5. several

1. untill
2. peice
3. could'nt
4. February
5. forty

1.
2.
3.
4.
5.

1. iceing
2. did'nt
3. theif
4. leaves
5. traitor

1. weigh
2. anser
3. cryed
4. haff
5. a lot

1. weird
2. slamming
3. adress
4. acter
5. aginst

1.
2.
3.
4.
5.

1. reccess
2. Wensday
3. height
4. victom
5. sword

1. tungue
2. dresser
3. tonite
4. around
5. beleif

1. aford
2. children
3. dawter
4. friend
5. seperate

1.
2.
3.
4.
5.

Seven-Up Spelling Cards

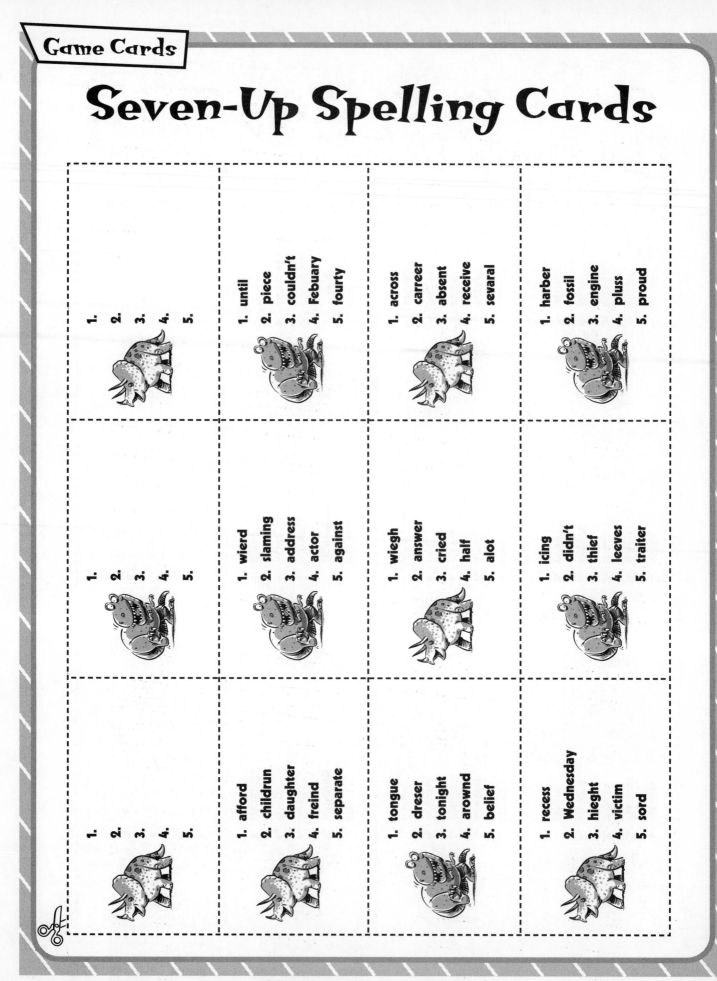

Card 1
1.
2.
3.
4.
5.

Card 2
1. until
2. piece
3. couldn't
4. Febuary
5. fourty

Card 3
1. across
2. carreer
3. absent
4. receive
5. sevaral

Card 4
1. harber
2. fossil
3. engine
4. pluss
5. proud

Card 5
1.
2.
3.
4.
5.

Card 6
1. wierd
2. slaming
3. address
4. actor
5. against

Card 7
1. wiegh
2. answer
3. cried
4. half
5. alot

Card 8
1. icing
2. didn't
3. thief
4. leeves
5. traiter

Card 9
1.
2.
3.
4.
5.

Card 10
1. afford
2. childrun
3. daughter
4. freind
5. separate

Card 11
1. tongue
2. dreser
3. tonight
4. arownd
5. belief

Card 12
1. recess
2. Wednesday
3. hieght
4. victim
5. sord

The Drop Deadline Grammar Slammer Game

Skill:

Proofreading and editing for grammar and spelling

Players:

Any number of teams of 2 to 4 players, plus a game monitor

Materials:

* Rules of the Game (page 90)
* Grammar Slammer Stories (pages 94–96)
* Practice Paragraph (page 92)
* Pencils
* Red pens or pencils
* Dictionary
* Clock or watch
* Answer Key (pages 92–93)

The Game in a Nutshell

In a fast-paced editing contest, teams correct as many grammar and spelling mistakes as they can in a newspaper article.

Preparation

Invite each team to choose a name, such as The Copy Chiefs or The News Hounds. Each team should elect officers:

* Editor-in-chief (leader)
* Copy editor (neatly marks all corrections on the final draft)
* Researcher (looks up words in the dictionary)
* Reader (reads copy in search of mistakes)

Choose one Grammar Slammer Story for everyone to edit. For each team, make two copies of the story—one for reading and making notes, and the other for making final corrections. Make a photocopy of the Rules of the Game for each team, and a transparency of the practice paragraph and the story.

Provide each team with a dictionary to look up spelling words, a pencil for proofreading, and a red pen or pencil for correcting final drafts.

Basic Grammar Skills

Deadline pressure at a newspaper is like being inside a balloon about to burst. Yet most editors stay cool, calm, and collected as they correct mistakes right up to the last minute. That's because these professionals know their grammar.

In this game, your students will get a taste of fast-paced newspaper editing. Mistakes will be made. Corrections will be missed. That comes with the job when you're on a "drop deadline." The goal is to see how clean each team can make its copy before "press time." (*Clean* means mistake-free. *Copy* is newspaper lingo for the text. *Press time* is when the newspaper must be ready to roll on the presses—no excuses, no delays.)

The Drop Deadline Grammar Slammer Game

All of the news stories provide practice with a mixed bag of errors (punctuation, spelling, subject-verb agreement, run-on or fragmented sentences, and so on), but each one emphasizes a different topic, such as spelling or verb tense. Each story contains 20 mistakes. The Answer Key lists the grammar points covered for each story.

To correct mistakes in any copy, students can simply cross out errors and write corrections either above the cross-out or in the right margin. However, proofreading marks will make their copy-edited drafts more professional. Review or introduce how to make these four basic ones:

- Triple underline turns a lowercase letter into an uppercase one:

  asia

- A carat (^) means to insert a word or punctuation mark:

  "Get rid it," he said.

- A delete mark is a line that crosses out the punctuation marks, letters, or words to be deleted and ends in a curlicue:

  "Your breathe reminds me of stale, rotten worms!"

  cried the elephant keeper.

- A snakelike line around two words or letters means to switch the order of the words or letters:

  She tried to swallow quickly.

Use the transparency of the practice paragraph to demonstrate how to make neat corrections. Important: Students should assume that people's names are spelled correctly. Other proper names, such as "american" in the practice paragraph, might need to be corrected.

Other Ways to Play

Kinder, Gentler Version: Allow unlimited time for teams to make corrections. The winner is the team (or teams) that makes the greatest number of proper corrections (up to 20 total).

Real-World Editing: Challenge students to play a variation of the "Grammar Slammer Game" with a real daily newspaper. Ask your local paper to donate a class set of yesterday's paper or have students bring newspapers from home. Working in teams, challenge students to find as many mistakes as they can on the front page of a section (news or sports, for example).

The Drop Deadline Grammar Slammer Game

Correct as many grammar and spelling mistakes as you can in a short newspaper article.

How to Play:

1. The game monitor will give you a story to edit. When the game monitor says, "Copy's in!" begin editing. Make all corrections in pencil.

2. When time is up, the game monitor will say, "Drop deadline!" Stop writing.

3. The game monitor will help you correct the story. You will earn one point for each correction you made. Insert any overlooked corrections in red pen or pencil on your draft. The team with the most points wins.

Players:
Any number of teams of 2 to 4 players, plus a game monitor

Materials:

* Grammar Slammer Story (from your teacher)
* Pencils
* Red pen or pencil
* Clock or watch

Practice Paragraph

There are four mistakes in this paragraph. Can you find and correct them?

Firefighters rescued Puffy again on Sunday. Puffy, an american tiger cat, were not injured. Firefighter Thad Smarts recieved several scratches and bruises they were painful.

Answer Key

Practice Paragraph

Capitalize *American; were* should be *was*; transpose *ie* in *received*; either split the last run-on sentence into two sentences or change the *they* to *that*. Remind students to assume that people's names such as "Thad Smarts" are spelled correctly. How many understand the pun ("that smarts")?

STORY 1: Spelling Bee
took [*verb tense*]
Bee [*capitalization*]
Runners-up [*plural*]
were [*sentence fragment*]
Justa Bout, [*punctuation*]
age 11 [*numeric spelling*]
change Capital to Capitol [*spelling*]
official [*spelling*]
office building [*capitalization*]
congress [*capitalization*]
change capitol to capital [*spelling*]
Washington, D.C. [*punctuation*]
cabbageworm [*spelling*]
deceive [*spelling*]
impair [*spelling*]
She didn't make one mistake. [*sentence
    fragment*]
misspelled [*spelling*]

disappointed [*verb tense*]
"I really wanted that trophy," she stated
afterward. [*punctuation*]
deserved [*spelling*]

STORY 2: Cookie Jar
was [*verb tense*]
reached [*verb tense*]
jar and [*punctuation*]
got [*verb tense*]
it [*pronoun agreement*]
mayor's [*possessive*]
assistant [*spelling*]
assistant, [*punctuation*]
assistance [*spelling*]
arrived [*verb tense*]
mayor [*capitalization*]
relieved [*verb tense*]
him [*pronoun agreement*]

deserve [*subject-verb agreement*]
medal [*homophone*]
medal," she said. [*punctuation*]
pulled [*verb tense*]
hand, [*punctuation*]
wasn't [*subject-verb agreement*]
hurt." [*punctuation*]

STORY 3: Sloths Beat Bunnies

Sloths [*plural, not possessive*]
Minneapolis [*capitalization*]
Minnesota's [*possessive*]
International [*capitalization*]
Snow, [*punctuation*]
North Pole [*capitalization*]
can't [*contraction*]
it's [*contraction*]
here [*homophone*]
It's [*contraction*]
Snow's [*possessive*]
dogs [*plural*]
received [*spelling*]
steak [*spelling*]
dinners [*plural*]
They're [*homophone*]
too [*homophone*]
It's [*contraction*]
race, [*compound sentence*]
we're [*contraction*]

STORY 4: Diva

Diva, a star singer, [*punctuation*]
mind: [*punctuation*]
beamed, [*punctuation*]
"simply [*capitalization*]
wonderful, [*punctuation*]
aren't [*contraction*]
Diva, who was born in Cleveland,
 [*punctuation*]
Cleveland [*capitalization*]
Angeles, home to many stars.
 [*sentence fragment*]
fabulous [*spelling*]
Diva will appear wearing gold and jewels on
a stage. [*misplaced modifier*]
jewels [*spelling*]
are [*subject-verb agreement*]
beautiful [*spelling*]
beautiful," Diva sighed. [*punctuation*]
too [*homophone*]
added. [*punctuation*]

fans, of which there are several,
 [*punctuation*]
agree," [*punctuation*]
Diva. [*punctuation*]

STORY 5: Student Teased

Mannerly, [*punctuation*]
don't [*contraction*]
write [*homophone*]
well [*adverb*]
well. I [*run-on sentence*]
a lot [*spelling*]
mistakes [*spelling*]
tease [*verb tense*]
me. What [*run-on sentence*]
I [*capitalization*]
do? [*punctuation*]
Everyone [*spelling*]
time to time [*punctuation*]
Even the people who tease you do.
 [*sentence fragment*]
Their [*homophone*]
being [*verb form*]
them [*pronoun*]
them. Just [*run-on sentence*]
studying [*verb form*]
truly, [*punctuation*]

STORY 6: Grammar Day

president [*capitalization*]
president, [*punctuation*]
urge [*spelling*]
Day [*capitalization*]
is [*sentence fragment*]
honorable [*spelling*]
their [*homophone*]
classrooms after a long winter of school
 [*sentence fragment*]
makes [*subject-verb agreement*]
mistake, [*punctuation*]
weeks [*plural*]
We, the students of Wordsworth Elementary
 School, [*punctuation*]
Elementary [*capitalization*]
We'll [*contraction*]
spellers [*spelling*]
You'll [*contraction*]
afterward [*spelling*]
Remember: [*punctuation*]
Vote [*capitalization*]
Day. [*punctuation*]

The Drop Deadline Grammar Slammer

Story 1: News
Champ Wins National Spelling Bee

Ima Champ, age 10, takes first place yesterday in the National Spelling bee. Runner-ups Camen Second, age 10, and Justa Bout age eleven. The contest was held in the Capital, the officiel Office Building of the U.S. congress. It is in the capitol city of Washington, DC.

Champ won by correctly spelling "cabageworm," "decieve," and "impare." Not one mistake. Camen Second mispelled only one word: "infinite."

Justa Bout was disappoint. "I really wanted that trophy she stated afterward. "I disserved it."

Story 2: News
Mayor's Hand Is Stuck in Cookie Jar

Earlier today, Mayor Lotta Money is in a real jam. She reaches into a cookie jar, and gets her hand stuck in them.

The mayors assistent Linda Hand, called for asistance. Minutes later, a firefighter will arrive to help the Mayor. Mayor Money was relieve to see it.

"Both Linda and the firefighter deserves a metal she said." "Together, they pulls the jar off my hand and I weren't even hurt.

Grammar Slammer

Story 3: Sports
Sloths Beat Bunnies

The St. Paul Sloth's beat the Mighty Bunnies of minneapolis in Minnesotas international Dog Sled Race. The winner, Crystal Snow won a free trip to the north pole.

"I cant wait to see if its as cold as hear," Snow said. "Its an honor to win."

Snows dog's recieved stake dinner's.

"Their hungry, to!" added Snow. "Its a long race and were all tired."

Story 4: Feature
Diva Discusses Herself

Oprah Diva a star singer has one thing on her mind; herself.

"I am," she beamed "Simply wonderful arent I?"

Diva who was born in cleveland lives in Los Angeles. Home to many stars.

"Los Angeles is," Diva gushed, "simply fabulus, isn't it?"

Diva will appear on a stage wearing gold and jewals.

"The gold and gems is beatiful Diva sighed." "I, to, am very lovely," she added

Her fans of which there are several agree.

"Of course they agree" said Diva, "I am simply the best."

Story 6: Opinion
Vote "Yes" on Grammar Day

As your student body President I erge you to support National Grammar day. The proposed date April 1.

On this honorible day, all students will come out of they're classrooms. After a long winter of school. If anyone make a grammar mistake it will mean six more week of school.

We the students of Wordsworth elementary School, need National Grammar Day. Well all be better writers and spelers. Youll thank me for it after ward. Remember; vote "yes" on National Grammar Day

Story 5: Column
Student Teased

Dear Miss Mannerly

I dont right so good I make alot of misteaks. Some people teases me what should i do

Sincerely,

Teased Out

Dear Teased Out,

Every one makes errors from time, to time. Even the people who tease you. They're mistake is be mean and rude to nice people such as you. Pay no attention to they just be yourself. Meanwhile, learn to write better by practicing and study.

Yours truly

Miss Mannerly